- THE DOCTOR IS IN -

DOCTOR NERDLOVE

DATING ADVICE

FOR THE MODERN NERD

- SINCE 2011 -

I Got Her Number... Now What?

A Geek's Guide to Texting, Snapchatting, and Sliding Into DMs

HARRIS O'MALLEY

Other Books By Harris O'Malley

It's Dangerous To Go Alone: A Relationship Survival Handbook

New Game + : A Geek's Guide to Love, Sex and Dating

When It Clicks: The Guide To Mastering Online Dating

Simplified Dating: The Ultimate Guide To Getting Better at Dating... Quickly!

Copyright © 2018 by Harris O'Malley

All rights reserved

No part of this book may be reproduced in any form or by any electronic or mechanical means, including information storage and retrieval systems, without written permission from the author, except for the use of brief quotations in a book review.

Book Layout & Cover Design: Tracy Lay / digivisualdesign.com

ISBN: 978-0-9963772-7-0

To the NerdLovers out there.
I couldn't do this without you all.

Contents

Foreword

Getting someone's number is one of the most time-honored traditions in dating. Getting that napkin with her number scrawled on it or having her enter her digits into your phone is almost like unlocking an achievement or coming home with a trophy. Sure, you could try to contact her the old-fashioned way — by stalking her social media until you find the right account[1] — but that's the mark of a loser. Getting her number is a sign of your dating prowess, the moment that separates the men from the boys and the desirable from the downtrodden who're going home alone. You and you alone have been chosen because you were smarter, funnier, more clever, or just plain more appealing than other folks who wanted to get with her.

How do you like them apples?

Of course, in this day and age, the Internet has become ubiquitous in our lives. Social media, instant messaging and Voice-Over-IP calling have given us an almost infinite number of ways of connecting with people.

---

1   Which is, in itself, the modern-day equivalent of calling every number with her last name in the phone-book and hoping you get lucky...

The problem is that, well, we now have an almost infinite number of ways of connecting with people.

We are connected to virtually everyone in the world through watches and phones and tablets... and we mostly use them to watch TV, stalk celebrities and argue with strangers about which superhero movies are the best.

But even in this age of constant connection, getting that invitation to talk with someone is still an incredibly intimate moment. You're being asked to step away from the crowd, to talk where it's just the two of you. In a real way, it feels as though you're moving up to the next level.

But then what? Where do you go from there? We are so used to communicating amongst virtual crowds that we almost get lost when it's just us. We have no real guidance, no codified system of best practices. Say what you will about the overly florid ways of writing letters to your intimates during the Victorian era, at least they had some rules to follow. As intimidating as calling someone might be, at least we all had some basic guidelines about when to call; after all, we hashed out that whole "three day" bullshit rule when *Swingers* was still fresh. But while we've moved on since then, the rules haven't kept up with the advances of time.

In a real way, it's still the Wild West out there, with different apps having entirely different cultures and social mores. As a result, there are a lot of conflicting ideas and a host of really bad practices that can snatch defeat from the jaws of victory

— and drive you insane in the process. How do you respond when you've sent that DM but the only response you get is the dreaded "..."? Or worse, a "read" notice, followed by deafening silence.

While texting and messaging is an incredibly powerful tool for flirting, building a connection, and getting dates, trying to navigate it can feel like a sink-or-swim situation and someone just tossed you an anchor.

But that's where I come in. As a dating coach — and someone who's been on more dates than he's had hot meals — I've lived through almost about every scenario in the book and I've been there to watch how dating has changed first hand. And while the medium may have changed, people haven't. Whether you're meeting somebody at a bar, trying to connect at a party, moving the conversation off of a dating app or simply trying to start a conversation over social media, getting somebody's number is about the search for a simple, human connection. Everything else is a distraction.

Once you understand this, everything else becomes clear. This is why women seem so much more fluent in text mediums; they understand the rules and structure that comes with texting because they are used to connection and conversation. Men spend too much time focused on the goal, and not enough on how to get there. As a result, they treat texting like the proverbial bull in the china shop, thrashing around because they don't know how they got there, how to maneuver or get out, all while causing huge mess in the process.

But the good news is: you can learn. And understanding the structure of communicating through text is like having a super power that most other guys will never have. Before we're through, you will learn:

- How to get her number
- How to get her attention (and keep it) when so many other men lose it
- How to maintain interest, and even build some intrigue and attraction
- How to stand out from a sea of other men who are begging for her time
- And how to turn those numbers into dates and relationships.

So take a deep breath, limber up your thumbs, and let's dive in.

CHAPTER 1

Talking With Our Thumbs, Like God Intended

*NerdLove's Law of
Emotional Momentum:*

**Emotions return to a neutral
state unless acted upon by an
outside force.**

Why do we text?

Back in the dark ages[1], if you wanted to talk to someone —
especially if you wanted to get a date — you had only one option:
you had to call them on the phone. This, for generations, was
an anxiety-producing nightmare, a punishment inflicted upon
the terminally shy and awkward. The tension and stress that
can come with calling someone on the phone — someone you're
attracted to, but don't have much of a social connection with —
can be almost unbearable.

Worse, talking over the phone gave you no time to think. You
were put on the spot and now you had to put up or shut up in
the moment. If you had a brain-fart and couldn't think about
what to say... well, now there's that awkward silence until one
of you drawls out the dreaded "Sooooo..."[2]

If the gods of dating were merciful and you got their voice mail,
then you had to communicate your intent in under a minute
and try to not sound like an idiot in the process. The anxiety of

1   Which is to say, the 1900s through the 1990s
2   Translated: "I'm just going to go now because this is clearly getting more
awkward by the second."

leaving a message is one that continues today, something we see reflected back to us in *Swingers, Singles, Community, He's Just Not That Into You* and more. You have to fight to resist the urge to delete the message and start over... provided that you don't just call back to try to explain the previous embarrassing message you just left.

Enter the miracle of the Short Message System. Sending text messages via cell phones had long been part of mobile networks, but the service came at a cost. Texting was expensive, particularly in the United States, where it was considered a premium service. Cellular providers would charge per text, or sell packages of so many texts per month. But as social adoption of SMS grew — alongside competition from Instant Messaging services — unlimited texting became part of the standard cellular service package. The number of text messages being sent grew by literal billions between 2003 and 2008. Texting became a central part of how we communicate with others.

And so it remains today.

In a world where we increasingly live our lives on social media, we do more and more communicating via text – through our smartphones, through Facebook and Twitter, through apps like Snapchat and WhatsApp and Kik. We are all increasingly connected to the network at all times. And the more connected we become, the more important texting becomes as a way to connect, flirt and date.

For many, texting is a godsend. There's never any question as to whether your message went through. Texting is inherently asynchronous, which means that you have time to think. There's less pressure to respond immediately, easing the anxiety of trying to be clever on the fly. Texting has even given us greater flexibility in the way we communicate. Emoji, memes, photos, Snaps, Instagram Stories, and animated gifs all convey levels of nuance and meaning in ways that even talking can't necessarily match.

Unfortunately, that also means a lot of people are doing it wrong. While texting can be a powerful tool for generating interest and getting dates, it's also the means by which you can snatch defeat from the jaws of victory. You have to use it correctly.

And that starts with understanding the reason why we text.

Remember the purpose of texting

One of the mistakes that many people make is that they forget the reason why we're texting, messaging and DMing people in the first place. We're communicating, yes, but we're communicating with a purpose.

How many of you have run into this common scenario: you met someone, you hit it off and now you're starting to message each other back and forth. But while the conversation is great at first, you're starting to get a weird feeling that something's gone wrong. At first, she was writing back almost as soon as you finished typing. Now she's taking longer and longer to reply. Five minutes. Ten minutes. Thirty minutes. Hours.

Worse, their responses are getting shorter and shorter. While you're as verbose as always, her replies have become increasingly terse. What started as paragraphs, even multiple texts in a series, have become single sentences. And then just words and symbols; emoticons and emoji, LOLs and "Yeah".

And then... nothing.

Now it's been a day, maybe two days. Maybe even longer. You're left wondering whether you should try to message her one more time or give her more time to get back to you. All you know is that a promising connection seems to have wasted away to nothing.

The reason why this happens so frequently is that people forget why we text women, or even why we asked for their number in the first place. We focus so much on details, that we forget the bigger picture. The reason why we're texting in the first place.

The whole point of getting someone's number and texting them is to actually meet up in person and go on a date. We aren't looking for friends, or texting buddies[3], we're looking for potential partners. As cold-blooded as it may sound at first, if

---

3   At least not yet, anyway.

---

you're not moving towards that goal, you're going to end up with radio silence or platonic friendships.

Don't get me wrong. This doesn't mean that you're trying to manipulate them or trick them. Nor does it mean that you're trying to avoid having awesome conversations or only ever push towards getting them out on a date. Quite the opposite, in fact. However, there is a specific dynamic that comes with texting someone you want to date, as opposed to texting a friend. When you lose that dynamic, you start to bleed away the interest and emotional momentum until there's nothing left. You go from being a potential partner to just somebody that she used to talk to.

If you want to avoid this, then you need to keep your head in the game. When it comes texting with an eye towards getting a date, there are three goals to keep in mind; everything else flows from them.

Goal #1: You Want Her To Respond When You Text Her

The first goal to successful texting is that you want her to respond to you when you text her. When you're pursuing a relationship with someone — whether it's for a lifetime or the next 30 minutes — the last thing you want is to be shouting into the metaphorical void. If that special someone never responds when you reach out, then nothing can ever happen. If they ignore you, or simply don't have a reason to reply, then the entire interaction dies.

But here's the thing: you aren't just trying to provoke a reaction from her. That's easy. Any jerk can do that. All you have to do is send something along the lines of:

> You: Hey did you know you're like a wrench?

Her: LOL what do you mean?

> You: Well, when I think about you my nuts tighten up.

Her: You asshole!

Needless to say: not the response you're hoping for.

One of the surprising issues that comes up around texting is how few men seem to understand that texting is a two way street. They put no effort into actually communicating. They start with a "hey" or "'sup" and nothing else. They reply to conversations with the hated "'k" or a seemingly random meme or emoji. They are are the conversational void — the place where communication goes to die and sexual and romantic excitement withers and fades into nothing.

Needless to say, this is counter to the goal of texting. The last thing you want is to kill her interest in you before it's even had a chance to come to life.

Texting, even if you're hoping to line up a hook-up, is a conversation. Conversations are like tennis; you serve the topic, they receive it and volley it back to you. "'sup", "hey" and the like do nothing to get the conversation started. It's the social equivalent of trying to volley a tomato over the net. It's going to land with a dull splat and just explode messily and all over the place.

And nothing is less sexy than a splattered tomato.

Remember: the purpose of texting is to lead to an actual date. If you can't start a conversation, that's not going to happen. "Hey," isn't the start of a conversation, it's a request for the person you're texting to be your conversational tour guide. At best, it's a sign that you don't have anything to say. At worst, you're telling them that you expect them to do most of the heavy lifting.

That's a pretty good sign that you aren't going to have much to offer her if you two were to meet up.

If you want to meet up in person, then you want her to respond to you when you text. If you want her to respond when you text, then you have to give her a reason to respond. You have to provide her with things to respond to, things she'll want to talk about with you. If there's no topic for her to latch on to, no compelling lure that entices her into talking to you, then you have failed at this goal. If you don't move the conversation forward, then you have failed.

Give her a reason to want to talk to you, not just to let your message sit at the bottom of her priority list.

Goal #2: You Want Her To Be Interested in You

The second goal seems obvious: you want to build and maintain her interest in you. After all, the reason you two exchanged contact information at first is because there was that initial spark of attraction. You dug her, she was into you, you both want to see where this could go.

The problem is, on their own, sparks are ephemeral things. Nurture them correctly, and a spark can be the the start of a lovely, roaring fire. Treat it the wrong way and that spark will just go out.

When it comes to texting, it's very easy to accidentally extinguish that initial spark of attraction. This is an area where many, many men fall down. They mistake being impressive for being attractive or aggressive for confident. More importantly, however, they don't understand the reason why we choose one person over another. It's not because they tick more boxes on a spreadsheet, because they have more money[4], the cooler job or the better body[5]. We pick the people we date because of how they make us feel.

Being able to make someone feel good is a vital component of attraction — and it's an important part of texting. We are attracted to people whose presence or behavior makes us feel appreciated and liked. This is known as The Reward Theory of Attraction. When someone's involvement in our lives makes us feel good, then we tend to be drawn towards that relationship over others. The brain increases dopamine and norepinephrine, which regulates the brain's pleasure and reward centers. We associate the pleasure with the person and thus want to spend more time in their presence.

This is why boredom is the most common attraction killer. Nine times out of ten, the reason why texting conversations fade away is simply because the excitement has faded. That thrill that came with meeting someone awesome dwindled away because there was nothing to maintain it. The conversations were nice enough, but nice isn't the same as exciting or engaging. Nice is pleasant, and pleasant is just... there. Those long, deep conversations over text or DM seem like a great way to build attraction. And they are... in person. Over text, however, they can become a bit much — especially when it's 90% of your interaction with someone.

---

4   Having lots of money is a great way to attract women... who are attracted to money. Not to you.

5   Physical attraction falls on a very large axis. People like a much wider variety of body types than our culture admits. And to quote Dita Von Teese: you can be the sweetest, juiciest peach out there, but some folks just don't like peaches.

Don't get me wrong: that sense of "We have these incredible conversations," is powerful. The sense that somebody gets you on a level that nobody else does helps create a powerful bond between people. But those conversations work best after you've had your first or second date. Until then, those conversations need to be mixed with reminders of why she was interested in you in the first place. You want to show that you can excite her, intrigue her, make her laugh and make her feel good.

The more you can get into somebody's head, the more you can get into her heart. The more she loves hearing from you, the more likely she is to want to date you.

Goal #3: You Want To Actually Meet Up

The third — and most important goal — of texting is very simple: you want to meet up in person.

Yes, this seems like it should be obvious. In practice however, people — men especially — get this wrong all the time. One of the eternal complaints of texting, regardless of gender, is how often it never goes anywhere. The conversations just go on and on and on.

And on.

And on...

Eventually somebody gets tired of waiting for that moment of "yes, let's do the thing!" and moves on to talk with someone who does seem interested in getting together in the flesh. Meanwhile, the other person is left wondering why yet another promising connection dried up on them.

I get why this happens. Asking somebody on a date means opening yourself up to rejection. You worry that they're not interested enough yet. You want to be sure — 110% sure, if not more so — that they're going to say yes. Or you worry that it's too soon and you're going to seem pushy or needy. Or you may be waiting for the right moment because, hell, what're you supposed to do? Just ask and give away that you're into them?

But here's something that nobody tells you: emotions have their own laws of physics, like physical objects do. And the excitement and attraction that you have at the start is no exception. Call it NerdLove's Law of Emotional Momentum: emotions return to a neutral state unless acted upon by an outside force. This is never more true than with excitement. Goal #2 can help keep that momentum going... for a little while. But it won't last forever.

So while you're hemming and hawing, their interest in you is starting to bleed away. By the time you've gotten yourself psyched up to actually ask them on a date, the excitement has faded and that eagerness to meet up with the had to see you lost it's luster. You may be a great guy, but you didn't do the one thing she needed from you: you didn't take the next step and propose an actual date.

If you don't want to watch yet another connection dwindle away to nothing, you need to keep the emotional momentum moving. You don't need to be asking for a date in every single conversation, but you do need to keep moving towards that goal. If you're not advancing the interaction, then all you're doing is pushing things towards the inevitable moment you realize that she's just not going to text you back.

She likes you. She wouldn't have given you their number if she didn't.

Ask her out already.

CHAPTER 2

Getting Her Number

The key to any interaction with someone you're hoping to date is to understand the ebb and flow of their feels.

Billy Don't Lose My Number

Before you can even begin to text someone, you have to get her number in the first place.

Getting a girl's number — or connecting on WhatsApp or Snapchat, for that matter — is a rite of passage. It's the moment of triumph after having met someone incredible at the bar. Maybe she put her number in your phone. Maybe she gave you the classic "number scrawled on a bar napkin". But as you walk away, "We Are The Champions" playing in your head, you have to remember:

The number doesn't count unless she's actually going to reply when you text or pick up when you call.

Something to keep in mind is that the fact that someone gave you their number doesn't mean that they were into you. Paradoxical, I know, but stick with me.

Even in this day and age, most women are socialized to be polite and to avoid hurting people's feelings — especially men's — even at the cost of their own. As a result, there are many times where women simply don't feel comfortable telling a guy "thanks, but no thanks." They may feel obligated to give their number to somebody who they're not actually interested in because it feels less rude than turning them down directly.

Other times, it's a way to end the interaction with someone who just won't get the hint. There are always guys out there who need to be hit across the face with a clue-by-four before they understand that someone really isn't into them. It's quicker to give somebody a number in order to make them feel like they've gotten somewhere and send him back to his bros.

However, there are also many men out there that take rejection badly. They hear a polite "no thank you", and start yelling about how the woman they were hitting on is really just a smelly pirate whore that they wouldn't bang with a borrowed dick. And that's if they don't get physical.

As a result, women often give *a* number — not always *their* number — in order to create a polite fiction that gets an otherwise sketchy dude out of their personal space.

Of course, as more guys caught on to the "give him a fake number" trick, they, in turn, would try to ensure that they had a working number by calling or texting immediately in lieu of giving theirs. But in the days of smartphones, burner apps, voice mail and caller ID, a phone number by itself is ultimately meaningless. Just because she didn't give you the number for the local cement processing factory doesn't mean that you're ever going to hear back from her.

On the other hand, it's also possible that she may just not remember who you are. This isn't a knock on you as a person; it's simply a matter of circumstance. In a loud, noisy and chaotic environment like a bar or a club, she may have vague memories of talking to someone she liked, but can't remember who. This turns a new name in her phone into a question of "wait, who was this guy again?" It's often less awkward to play "new phone, who's this?" games than it is to admit that you don't remember somebody. Similarly, if she was having a wild night out, with lots of alcohol involved, she may feel embarrassed by her actions the cold light of sobriety. Many a number has been deleted because of a panicked sense of "Oh God, what did I do?" rather than a lack of interest.

Needless to say: you don't want any of this to happen. You want to make sure that you not only get her contact information, but that you can also be assured that she will be happy to hear from you when you message her and — as per Goal #1 — that she'll actually respond.

Picking Your Moment

One of the reasons so many men fail at getting a phone number — or any other form of contact, for that matter — is because they go about it the wrong way. They push too hard, too quickly and trigger the "make this guy go away" feeling. Or they take too long and ask for a phone number long after the moment has passed. Worse, they wait so long that someone has to leave, and now there's that last minute scramble of "Wait, will I see you again?!?" that ends with someone kicking themselves for missing a beautiful opportunity.

And of course, there's the simple question of "If you get her number, will she text you back?"

So let's talk tactics about how to get somebody's number, in a way that all but guarantees that she'll be dying to hear from you.

First, of course, you have to actually ask for her number. If you've been having a solid conversation with someone — where you've had plenty of back-and-forth and everybody is participating equally, instead of one person doing all the talking as the other just makes polite "I'm listening, no really..." noises — for 15 to 20 minutes, there's no reason not to ask. That conversation is a good indication that you two have some solid chemistry together; it's completely natural to want to keep the conversation going elsewhere — or to see each other again.

At this point, it's just a matter of picking your moment. This can feel like a monumental task, but it's much easier than you realize. The key is to wait for (or trigger) a spike of positive emotions.

In fact, the key to any interaction with someone you're hoping to date is to understand the ebb and flow of their feels. No matter how much you may be into each other, your emotional states are going to have peaks and valleys — high points of excitement and energy followed by a dip and return to the baseline.

This happens all the time. Think of any conversation you've had with friends. You start with the natural resting state of your conversation, punctuated with moments where you both get revved up and excited before you return to that initial base level. Those emotional highs can vary; it may be because one of you told a joke and cracked you both up, it may be the end of an awesome story or even just something cool that happened while you were both watching the game on TV.

Those emotional highs are the key to moving any interaction forward because of a couple quirks of human psychology.

The first is what's known as the "Misattribution of Arousal". Humans are bad at understanding why we feel the way that we feel. We feel the physical sensations of an emotion and backfill a reason for why we feel them based on what's going on around us. When our hearts are pounding, our palms are sweaty and our mouths go dry, we may be afraid... or we may be aroused. It all depends on the context; if we see a leopard in the grass, then obviously we're afraid. But if we see someone hot instead, then clearly we're aroused instead. So when we have those emotional highs that make us feel awesome, we tend to attribute them to the people around us — even if it was caused by someone else.

This is important because it feeds into the second quirk: The Reward Theory of Attraction from Goal #2. The more that she associates those positive feelings with you, the more she's going to want to hear from you and get that dopamine hit.

This makes those emotional spikes the perfect time to ask for somebody's number; you're surfing the crest of the wave of good feelings and establishing that you are the person who's made them feel incredible. Understanding this dynamic means that you'll know how to pick your moment and — importantly — establish yourself as the person she wants to hear from.

When you've caused that positive spike, or recognize when one is happening, you're going to make your move. And you're going get her number by using a particular technique known as pre-seeding.

"This Is The Phone Number You're Looking For"

Remember what I said about the three goals of texting? This is an example of how keeping those goals in mind is what leads to an actual date. While you're talking to somebody you're into, you want to sow the potential of a date. You're going to talk about future plans — ideally, something you're doing anyway[6] — that you're really looking forward to. It could be an art exhibit.

6   This has less to do with any social games and more with feeling relaxed and natural; it's easier to sell someone on going with you to something you enjoy than it is to try to come up with an idea on the fly.

It could be going to the zoo, or it could be a band you're excited to see. The specifics matter less than the fact that you're talking about something that you care about.

Then, when you hit that perfect moment — that positive spike of emotions — you ask her out on a date.

Here's what it looks like:

"Hey, can I be real here? I'm having a really great time talking to you."

"Thanks, me too."

"You know, I'm doing $COOL_THING later this weekend and I think you'd really enjoy it. I'd love to take you."

"Yeah, I'd really like that."

"Great, tell you what, let me get your number..."

And then you hand her your phone.

If you've been paying attention, you can see how the Three Goals weave together here. First, you're affirming those good feelings; telling her "Hey, I'm having a great time," is a subtle way of asking her to agree with you that yes, you're having a good time together. This reinforces Goal #2: she feels good talking to you and is more likely to want to see you again.

Next, you're giving her a reason to want to reply when you text her: you're planning a date together. At the bare minimum, you're going to work out the logistics of the date. But planning that date — and the excitement of doing something cool with the awesome guy she just met — is going to keep that interest alive and make her eager to see you again, nicely fulfilling Goals #1 and #3.

Making solid plans is crucial. Too many men will phrase the invitation as "Let's get together some time" or "I'd love to hang out, let me know." This is, frankly, a weak move. It's wishy-washy at best, and it puts the onus of actually inviting someone on a date on the other person. While there are lots of women out there who have no problem being the one taking the initiative, being asked to do so — in a passive-aggressive way, at that — is a little insulting. If you're into somebody, own your attraction and ask them on a date. Putting it on them is just crass and unattractive.

Of course, not every conversation you're going to have with someone you're into is going to naturally lead to an opportunity to ask someone for a date. It's hard to pre-seed a date idea at a concert, for example, or a loud bar. Alternately, you just may not feel like the time is right. You may even feel a little intimidated. That's fine. You just change the way you ask for the number:

"Hey, I have to tell you, I'm having a really great time talking to you."

"Thanks, I am too!"

"I'd love to keep this going/see you again

— is it cool if I get your number?"

"Yeah, I'd really like that."

Now, if asking for her number feels as though it is a step too far, then ask to add her on WhatsApp, Snapchat or whichever messaging app you both use instead. However, a phone number is preferable for a specific reason: it's higher on the intimacy ladder.

Understand The Intimacy Ladder

One of the keys to texting with an eye towards dating is to remember that different communication apps and methods have different cultures. It's not unusual to find yourself having two entirely different types of conversation on Twitter and Facebook for example, or Snapchat and WhatsApp... even though it's with the same person. Some of this is simply based on the structure of the app; Twitter's 280 characters lends itself to short, pithy snippets, while Snapchat is more designed for back-and-forth photos with cute stickers and text. Tumblr promotes conversations through reblogging with commentary, Instagram lends itself to more declaratory posts, and Facebook is now predominantly the domain of the Olds: grandmas and Gen-X-ers who don't keep up with the latest trends.

Similarly, talking on the phone may be stressful and to be avoided, but hanging out on video chats in Skype is common among friends.

But not only are there cultural differences, there are different levels of intimacy to the many ways we communicate now. As I've mentioned in my book *New Game +: The Geek's Guide To Love, Sex and Dating*, the way you communicate with someone is, in many ways, indicative of what level of intimacy you have with them. Some methods of communicating are the online version of talking at the bar or a party — where there is no expectations of privacy or intimacy — while others are reserved for close friends and potential dates.

While the order can vary from person to person, there's a general ladder of implied intimacy in how you communicate with someone.

From most intimate to least, it goes:

- 👤 In Person
- 📞 Phone
- 💬 Text
- 😊 Video Chatting (including Skype and FaceTime)
- 💻 Direct Messaging (DMs on Twitter, Instagram, Facebook Messenger)
- ✉️ E-mail
- ⚡ Instant Messaging (WhatsApp, Snapchat, Kik, etc.)
- 👍 Facebook/Instagram/Twitter

It's worth noting that despite how we increasingly live our lives online — sharing so much about ourselves on Facebook and Instagram, communicating on social media is actually less personal... at least when you're commenting on somebody's posts and pictures. While you can have epic-length conversations in the comments, it's still the social equivalent to talking to somebody in a public space. This is why it's incredibly awkward and uncomfortable when your uncle goes off on a racist rant on a post about politics... or when some thirsty dude starts drooling over somebody's selfies. It's as though they're acting like this in a crowded restaurant.

Direct messaging on social media apps, on the other hand is considerably more intimate; it's like being taken aside for a private conversation, where it's just the two of you.

In an ideal world, you want to be moving up the intimacy ladder — see Goal #3. However, it's worth noting that you're likely to bounce around on the ladder, especially in the early days. After all, people talk on multiple systems. If you're friends with someone on Facebook and you follow them on Twitter, and you have their number, you may be texting and using Facebook Messenger and posting snarky memes at one another on Twitter. Your place on the ladder is at the highest level that you can reasonably expect a response on. So if you email back and forth regularly but also text on occasion, you can assume that you're at the higher level of intimacy. And, of course if you're meeting in person on the regular, then you are as likely to message on any and all platforms.

However, dropping down ladder — she responds to your voicemails with texts, for example, or she stops responding to your texts but will still occasionally like your posts on Instagram — is a sign that you've made a mistake along the way. Moving down the ladder is an indicator that she doesn't feel as comfortable with you, and the way you communicate has been downgraded accordingly. The fact that she's still occasionally commenting on things you post on Facebook means that she's not quite ready to completely cut you out.

Yet.

Continuing to communicate in an open forum like public-facing social media is a polite way of staying in touch, but without the expectation of intimacy and emotional closeness that comes with a more private form of communicating. It's performative politeness for politeness' sake. If this is a regular pattern and you've been steadily dropping down the ladder — or even skipping rungs entirely — then you're now in damage control mode and the odds are high that she's going to go radio silent on you.

Similarly if the two of you have been texting back and forth and she starts to call you instead, it's a very good sign — and an indication that you should be asking her out on a date already.

Remember: stay aware of where your interactions are on the intimacy ladder and keep trying to move upwards. After all, if you don't meet in person, you aren't going to actually be able to date, hook up or otherwise move things in the direction you're hoping for.

CHAPTER 3

The Fundamentals of Texting

Remember: the ultimate goal here is to see her in person. Boring conversations won't get you there.

Let's Talk about Text, Baby...

Men often assume that there's a secret trick to texting for success. They want to know what to send that will guarantee a response, what they can send that will make her come over for a bootie call (even if she's not that kind of girl) or ensure that she won't flake.

As long as you're wishing, you may as well ask for winning Powerball tickets while you're at it.

The fact of the matter is, texting isn't magic. It's not a secret way of bypassing her conscious mind or getting her to do things she might not do otherwise. It's not math or computer programming, where using the exact same formula will get you the exact same result each and every time. Humans don't work like that, no matter what the marketing hype may tell you.

Texting is *conversation*. The fact that you're using words on a screen instead of speaking in person doesn't change this. Neither does the use of emoji, memes, Instagram Stories, Snaps, DMs, or semaphore for that matter. If you aren't a great conversationalist, then you're not going to be much better at texting.

You want to treat text the way that you would treat talking to somebody in person or on the phone. The only difference is that texting is asynchronous; your conversation may be spread over time, instead of an immediate back and forth. The same things that bore women and drive them away when you're talking to them at a party will be the exact same things that bore them when you're texting.

Now, with that having been said, there *are* dynamics that are relatively unique to texting — especially when you're texting with an eye towards dating someone. After all: humans are built for face to face communication; certain nuances get lost when we can't hear people's voices or see the expressions on their face.

If you want to turn a phone number into an actual *date*, then you need to keep the fundamentals of texting in mind. And the first fundamental rule of texting is simple...

Be Sure She Remembers You

One of the most important rules when it comes to texting is the most obvious: you need her to remember who you are.

How many times do you see people in your timeline in Facebook or in your contacts on your phone and not remember who they are or how you ended up with their number? How many names on your phone are from incredibly weak connections — people you only vaguely remember talking to once or twice at a party, but took their number anyway?

Now imagine this from the perspective of an attractive woman. If she's especially social, she may have met many other people on the same day that you asked for her number. Moreover, if you've waited to contact her, that initial sharp impression of you may have blurred and faded to a vague memory.

This isn't a knock on you — or her, for that matter. It's just one of the limits of the human brain; if we don't need the information immediately, it gets shuffled off to another sector in the drive, where it won't get accessed as easily or as often.

This is why it's on *you* to make sure she remembers who you are. You want to make sure you stand out in her memory in order to avoid the dreaded: "new phone, who this?"

It's important that you do this as quickly as possible. Having a conversation with a stranger who clearly knows *you* is uncomfortable and awkward — two things you want to avoid if you're hoping to turn a phone number into an actual date. The longer it takes for her to remember who you are and why you have her number, the weirder it gets.

At the same time however, you want to do so with more class and grace than something awkward like

> Hey, it's Jake,

Um... right?

> We met two nights ago at The Library,

Wait, were you the one who knocked over that table?

> No, I was wearing the Doctor Who shirt, you asked about the show?

I guess?

This is one of the reasons why I'm a big believer in texting soon after you get the number; not just so you can do the "trade texts, here's my number" dance, but so that you cement yourself in their mind early on.

Speaking from personal experience: depending on how and where I met someone, I would often text within 20 minutes. The exact text would on the vibe of the conversation we had been having. If we were having a more quippy, banter-y conversation, it might be a "Holy crap, you won't believe what you missed after you left" text. If we were being flirtier, it might be something along the lines of "It was great meeting you, BTW, I wanted to tell you you have an awesome smile; sorry I was too shy to tell you in person."

Another good first text is to come back to something you two talked about when you met. For example: often when I'm flirting with someone, I'll ask what are known as "open questions" as a way of sparking conversation. An open question is one that can't be answered with a "yes" or a "no", but can lead in any number of different directions, depending how she answers. Personally, I prefer to ask questions about pop-culture, especially movies or music.

> "Hey, do you know who sang that song... something about about 'under the milky way' or some such? I keep confusing it with this song about Keith Moon..."

Or

> "Hey, who was that actress in Ghost World, not Scarlett Johansson the other kind of geeky goth one? She kind of reminds me of you..."

These questions provide not just a pretext to text them, but helps cement who you are and how they met you, right off the bat.

For example:

> "Hey $NICKNAME, I did some Googling and it turns out that the band we were talking about was The Church..."

However, one of the best ways to remind someone of who you

are is to use callback humor. This is an incredibly powerful way of reminding someone of who you are, and one that can be modified to fit your particular personality. This includes:

- 💡 Using a nickname that reminds her of something you two talked about.
- 💡 Referencing a joke the two of you shared while you were talking
- 💡 Bringing up fun or crazy things you two saw or did together — things that make you memorable in a good way.[7]

This serves two purposes. First: it's an easy way to remind them of who you are. People are more likely to remember the wacky things that happened or the silly nickname you gave each other than they are if you text them like you were writing a Missed Connection post on Craigslist.

Second: it makes them laugh. Being able to make someone laugh puts you ahead of the pack when it comes to attraction.

Most guys are dull and predictable and about as exciting as dry toast. Someone who can make her laugh is someone she'll appreciate hearing from. Why? Well, I'm glad you asked, convenient rhetorical device...

7   After all, the last thing you want is to remind her that you're the guy who spilled a drink on her favorite blouse or accidentally insulted her dog...

...though that can work, if you were able to recover from it in a cool way.

Focus on Her Emotions

Attraction is an emotional state. Unless you're a Vulcan or a medieval noble trying to arrange an advantageous marriage for your heir, people don't date based on logic. We don't look at potential partners on a spreadsheet, tally up their pluses and minuses and pick whomever has the highest score; we date the people we *like*. We date the people who hit that primal part of us, that mammalian core of our brain that ignores logic and focuses on how we feel when we're around them.

This is why when you're trying to get someone to date you, you don't want to have dull, unexciting conversations. Too many men treat texting less as a method of flirting and more as a way to just keep reminding women that they exist. Too many conversations start like this:

> Hey, how's it going?

OK, I guess. What are you up to?

> Not much, u?

You've seen these conversations. You likely have had many of them. These sorts of conversations are attraction killers. They are the Anti-Sex Equation. All they do is waste time and provide nothing of value. Not only is it boring, but it carries the unspoken message of "I am bored and I want you to entertain me." When you send a text like this, you're telling women that you're hoping that *they* will be the conversational events coordinator because *you* aren't bringing anything to the table.

This is why if you're going to text someone you want to date, you need to remember: you aren't trying to get into her pants, you're trying to get into her head. You want to show that you can make her feel good.

The easiest way to do that is to focus on her emotions. When she hears the ping of an incoming text message and gets the notification that you just messaged her, you want her to be eager to see what you've had to say.

This is especially true when you're texting someone you've just met. Establishing that you're entertaining and fun to talk to is a great way to get them invested in you.

To give a personal example: I once met a girl wearing a painted cowboy hat at a coffeeshop. Over the course of our conversation, we made various flirty jokes about the hat, ropes and riding cowboys, culminating with turning her hat around and saying that now she was a reverse cowgirl[8]. After getting her number, our first text exchange went something like this:

> What's up, Reverse Cowgirl?

Oh God I was hoping you forgot that. *-_-*

> Nope, not going to forget someone who knows the proper way to rock a hat...

Careful you, I can still hog-tie you in 10 seconds flat.

....

8   Google it, kids.

Within three exchanges, not only have I reminded her of who I was, but also the flirty fun we'd had when we met, and got her laughing and playing along. Now not only is the conversation rolling, but we can go any number of directions; we can flirt, we can trade jokes, we talk about wacky things we're up to.

But the most important part is that I put my focus on affecting her emotionally and providing value by helping her feel just a little bit better by providing that laugh.

There are any number of ways that you can affect someone's emotions in a positive manner when you're texting. Humor is an obvious example; women love a man who can make them laugh for a reason, after all.

Another option is to inspire her curiosity — few things can get somebody's interest quite as quickly as "you won't believe what happened to me today."

Alternately, engage her empathy or sense of compassion or cuteness by sending her a text that will make her say "awwwww". Tell her you saw something adorable and had to share or, even better, share a photo or video of said cuteness. It doesn't need to be something you actually saw in person — there're plenty of cute animal Tumblrs and YouTube channels out there — it just needs to trigger her positive emotions and make her squee from the cuteness.

Keep in mind: because texting is asynchronous, you have time to think about what you want to say. In fact, you can actually give yourself an advantage by preparing things in advance. I have an album of photos and memes on my phone *specifically* for sending to people to start conversations and and make them laugh.[9]

Now, not every conversation can be a laugh riot, nor can you just joke your way into someone's pants. You *are* going to have to be serious at times; dealing with someone who's *always* joking is exhausting. But do your best to keep dull conversations to a minimum... especially when you haven't even had your first date.

Beware Being Misunderstood

One of the hardest things to convey via text is nuance. Humans are designed for face to face communication. While we use words to talk, we change the meaning and impact of those words with body language, vocal intonation, facial expressions, even where we happen to be right at that moment.

Take the phrase "God, I hate you so much." Written out like that, it sounds harsh. If you got that text that from someone you cared about, you'd be understandably hurt. But if someone were to

---

9   Admittedly, it does help to live in a city where you'll regularly see things like helper monkeys playing with steering wheels at stoplights or people riding horses through urban neighborhoods.

say that to your face, you would have reams of information that would affect how you interpreted their meaning.

Were they saying it with a smirk and a wry tone of voice? Then they were likely being ironic or sarcastic. Did they say it with a roll of their eyes and an exasperated tone? Then in all likelihood they were expressing frustration or irritation. Was their face red and they screamed it at you? Then... well, they're probably telling you exactly how angry they were.

None of these cues exist when it comes to text. All you have is how well you can "read" the other person's tone. If you don't know them well — or even if you do — then you run the risk of drastically misunderstanding them.

This risk runs both ways; the funny gag you send that you're 100% convinced couldn't possibly be seen as anything other than a joke could be taken at face value. I've seen relationships fall apart because somebody didn't understand their partner's "clever" quip and ended up having their feelings hurt so badly that the relationship couldn't survive.

There are ways of conveying nuance and meaning in modern texting. Most of them tend to be non-verbal. Emoji, for example, can help give context to a message that could otherwise be misunderstood. Adding a 🙂 to a seemingly mean text can make it clear that you're not serious. Memes, animated GIFs, messaging app stickers, even short video clips can all carry information that ultimately changes the meaning of a text or message.

However, even these aren't fool-proof. Sticking a smiley face at the end of something mean doesn't make it not hurt — especially if you happen to be accidentally stepping on that person's emotional landmine.

This is why you need to be incredibly careful when you're texting someone, especially someone you're only just starting to get to know. Sarcasm and playful "meanness" can be taken seriously, while self-deprecating humor often comes across as beating yourself up for sympathy. Some jokes, gags or pranks are best avoided until you and your partner know each other very well.

In the early days of texting someone, do your best to be as up front and clear as possible. It's better to err on the side of being earnest and straightforward, than to end up killing a burgeoning attraction with a joke that went badly.

Understand When You're Being Ignored

I get it. You really want to hear back from that sexy someone you just met. But your texts, your calls, your emails, pokes and DMs are all just disappearing into the void and you're not sure what it means.

Well, I'll tell you what it means. It means that they don't want to talk to you.

Here's the handy rule of thumb:

One unreturned text could be anything. They're busy. They're at work and their boss is nearby. They're focused on something else at the moment.

Two unreturned texts is concerning, but understandable. Their phone may be dead, they may be at a movie, they may be up to their eyeballs in work or the phone's in another room.

Three unreturned texts is ~~enemy action~~ a message. And that message is "I'm not interested."

The three text rule isn't an iron-clad absolute. Sometimes shit happens and they just haven't gotten back to you. However, don't make the mistake of thinking that you can just jump mediums and reset the clock. You don't get three unreturned texts by phone and three unreturned emails and three unreturned Instagram DMs. You get three unreturned messages, period. And if the return message drops down the Intimacy Ladder? Well, you know what that means: you're in damage control mode.

Incidentally, don't ask if they got your text.

They did.

They just don't want to reply.

Have A Reason To Text

In the early days, texting conversations should be like a knife: it should be short, sharp and have a point. This is especially true when you're texting someone before you've had your first date. Texting someone you're into without a plan is a rookie mistake. This is how you end up with conversations to nowhere that end up dwindling away into nothing.

If you're going to text somebody, you need to have a reason behind it — something more involved than just "I want to talk to her" or "I want to remind her that I exist." These are noble goals, don't get me wrong... but they tend to lead to boring conversations that go nowhere and leave you running the risk of draining away any attraction you'd built up previously.

Starting any conversation with any variation of "What's up?" or that could be answered with "not much, u?" is a both boring and a great way to fade into the background noise of somebody's day. There's no meat there, there's no real reason to want to text back and it sounds almost exactly like the same texts that she's gotten from other, less interesting guys.

Worse, there's nowhere to go from there but down.

If you're going to text somebody, have a reason to do so —

preferably something that helps you advance the Three Goals of Texting. These don't need to be elaborate plans; you're trying to get a date, not outwit Batman and plunge Gotham City into chaos. But you need to have a point to texting them other than just "remind them I'm alive".

Are you trying to get their attention and make sure they'll write back? Cool, then do something that will affect her emotions. Have a funny event that you need to share or an idea you want to bounce off of her.

Are you trying to maintain emotional momentum? Good, then don't bore her to tears, give her a reason to remember why they want to see you.

Are you trying to lead up to getting a date? Great... then ask her on a date.

Remember: the ultimate goal here is to see her in person. Boring conversations won't get you there.

The benefit of texting is that you've got time to plan. You're not standing there awkwardly, trying to find something to fill the empty air. Put some thought into what you're going to say before you hit "send".

Always Be Closing

So I get it. You, like many people, want to try to minimize the odds of getting shot down when you ask someone out for a date. You want to maximize the possible attraction between the two of you.

Too bad. You're on the clock, my dude, and there's no way to completely eliminate the risk of rejection. There's no magic trick to making sure that somebody won't turn you down. You're going to have to roll the dice sooner or later.

And honestly? You're better off going with "sooner".

You need to keep NerdLove's Law of Emotional Momentum in mind. The longer you go between getting a number and getting a date, the more excitement bleeds away and the more you risk getting to the point that they just won't return your messages at all.

Getting to know each other is great; it's part of how you find out how compatible you are and leads to long, wonderful relationships. But texting is a bad way to do it, especially when you haven't had your first date yet. The best way to get to know each other? Go on a date and talk in person.

The other thing to keep in mind: the odds are that you aren't the only person who wants to date her. One of the realities of dating is that people aren't waiting around for one person to make up their mind about whether they're going to make a move or not.

Whether you met in person or on a dating app, most people — women in particular — are talking to more than one person at a time.

This doesn't mean that you're in competition; like I said earlier, we don't date based on spreadsheets and scores, we date based on who we like and who likes us. However, what can often make the difference between one person getting a date with a hottie and the other having another night at home alone playing Fortnite is that the former actually asked her out on a date and the other person didn't.

Straight talk: it doesn't matter how much someone likes you if you never actually make a move. Yes, they could ask *you* out but the hard truth is that even in the 21st century, gender roles are still a thing, a lot of women feel weird about being the aggressor and a lot of guys don't react well to women taking the initiative.

And let's be honest here: if she wasn't at least a little interested in you, she wouldn't have given you her number, nor would she be replying when you message her.

The longer you wait to actually make a move towards getting a date, the more likely it is that you'll never actually get that date.

This is why you need to remember Goal #3 and always be moving towards meeting up in person. When you text, do so with the intention of asking her out to do a specific date at a specific time and place. Not to "hang out some time", not to "get together", but to go do something.

Remember, this isn't a case of your trying to backdoor your way into a relationship with someone by pretending to be their strictly platonic friend[10] and letting them know you're interested might scare them away. You don't earn cool points by acting as though you don't think they're cute and hiding the fact that you like them. You got their number because you're interested in them romantically.

So act like it.

If you're going to text, text with a purpose.

A, B, C, motherfuckers. Always Be Closing.

---

10 Seriously, this is a shitty thing to do to someone. Never do this.

CHAPTER 4

The Do's And Don'ts of Flirting Via Text

It's very easy to overstay your welcome in a [text] conversation with someone, and this is a great way to ensure that you'll never actually see them in person.

Keep The Flirting Light Until After Your First Date

There are many things to keep in mind when it comes to the best practices regarding flirting via text. It's a subtle art, and one that's easier to get wrong than it is to get right. But when you do get it right, then flirting via text can be an incredibly powerful tool in your social arsenal.

But whether you're texting someone after having gotten their number, or you're trying to slide into someone's DMs, you need to follow certain guidelines and best practices to make texting work for you.

First and foremost is that you don't want to try to use text as a way to build attraction; not when you haven't had your first date yet. Remember, your goal is to try to get that date, not just keep having great or deep conversations. The longer you take to actually go out on a date, the more you're losing emotional momentum.

Texting can keep things moving, but it's no substitute for face to face interaction. Flirting works best when you've met in person because you have far more to work with — from touch to tone of voice, to being able to incorporate your surroundings or activities into your flirting.

Just as importantly, however, is that flirting via text is much easier when you have that previous history of having been together in person. When you're flirting after having met at least once, you're making a more seamless transition, taking your shared experiences and bringing with you into a different medium.

Trying to jumpstart flirting with someone you have only just met — or have never met in person — is slightly more jarring. It can be done — Tinder and OKCupid base their entire business model around this after all — but it can feel less organic and less natural. This is especially true depending on the context of the medium. Flirting is expected behavior when it comes to using Tinder; it's not part of the implied social contract on, say, Twitter or Instagram. Having someone you don't know try to start a private conversation and getting flirty and sexual immediately can be an unpleasant experience. In many cases, it's more like having someone catcall you on the street, rather than a suave individual capturing your attention with their wit and charm.

Don't forget that while being a texting guru is admirable, unless you're just looking for a sexting buddy, your focus should be on getting that first date. Otherwise, you're just tossing words out into the void.

By all means, do flirt during the lead up to your date. But don't put all your efforts into building attraction via text; you're better off to work towards getting a date, not trying to grind your social meter with her.

After you have that first date, however, texting becomes vital. Knowing how to keep a woman's interest, build some intrigue and even some excitement, is part of how you take a great first date and ensure you have a second. And then a third.

Don't Be Predictable

Most guys out there are horrible at texting. In fact, any woman who's been dating for a while can tell you: there are far too many dudes out there who bring nothing to the conversational table. Date enough of them and you can practically write the script yourself like a social Nostradamus.

You want to stand out from the pack of average, uninteresting guys and bring your a-game. Where everyone else is boring them with the standard "'sup?", you are going to zig where others zag and keep her on her toes.

To do this correctly, you need to remember Goal #1: you want to get her to respond. Surprise is easy; any hack can shock someone. You want to intrigue her. You want to pique her interest and get her to write back or play along.

So instead of the standard logistics questions — what's up, how's your day going — you are going to make statements instead. These are going to be things that prompt a follow-up because she's just going to have to know.

For example:

> I try to keep an open mind, but I think the woman who brought her emotional support llama to the coffeeshop today may be abusing the system.

or

> Before today I didn't know that you could have seeing-eye horses.

or

> Hey I just saw your evil twin.

Alternately:

> Either you were at the same restaurant as me at breakfast and didn't say hi or you have a secret clone and it's kind of weirding me out.

or

> I had a weird dream about you wearing a koala suit so I just wanted to say "hi". And "stay out of my dreams".

Part of what makes these useful is that not only do these beg for a response, but you can take the conversation off into almost any direction. You can have a follow-up that plays off what you'd just said — "Yeah, turns out your evil twin really knows how to rock a goatee" — or you branch off into a new topic.

Another option is to send a text that starts an interesting (but not serious) conversation — something that invites a whimsical debate.

For example:

> What is the superior kid's cereal?

or

> What toppings do not belong on pizza?

or

> Which are cooler: pirates or ninjas?

or

> Who'd win in a fight: an astronaut or a caveman?

or

> Do you prefer to avoid spoilers or do you go looking for them?

or

> **If you had your choice of super powers, would you rather have mind reading or flight?**

Now keep in mind: you're not going full Dadaist here, nor do you need to be as wacky as some of these suggestions may sound. The goal is simply to be a little surprising and get a fun conversation started, not come across as a visitor from Cloud Cuckoo Land.

That having been said, tone is important. Why? Because the next tip:

Keep Things Playful

One of the important parts of dating, especially when you're still working towards those first dates, is that it's supposed to be fun. The more someone enjoys hearing from you or spending time in your presence, the more they're going to want to spend time talking with you.

This is why your flirting should be light and playful, especially when you're in the early stages of getting to know somebody. Part of why I suggested some slightly off-beat texts is because they set a certain tone within the interaction; they're silly and fun and encourage a similar response from the person you're texting with.

No matter how intense and immediate that initial attraction may be, you want things to feel light and fun and easy. Those long, deep and meaningful conversations are great... but they're better saved for in person, and ideally after you've had a few dates. Otherwise, you run the risk of triggering a nebulous sense of "they're interesting, but this doesn't feel like attraction to me".

There are any number of ways that you can maintain this playful flirtation. One method is to use light teases in your texting. How this works can depend on the personalities involved. Some people like a slightly antagonistic style of flirting — giving one another playful shit as it were. Think Nick and Nora from *The Thin Man*, Donna and Josh from *The West Wing* or Bob and Linda Belcher from *Bob's Burgers*. The teasing is gentle and done with affection rather than meanness.

Another is to play around with expectations. A great way to set this dynamic is to send something like this:

> Hey $NICKNAME, can you keep a secret?

Of course I can!

> Great, so can I... ;)

This will, in all likelihood, get a groan. After all, it's a bit predictable and silly. But unless she's had her sense of fun surgically removed at a young age, it will at least get a smile with the groan.

You can even be a bit naughty with your flirting as long as you keep things light and focus more on innuendo than outright sexiness.

For example:

> You just gave me a really inappropriate thought just now, and I really don't know you well enough for that yet.

or

> Oh man, what am I going to do with you? I mean I have some ideas, but they're really not ok yet.

or

> Hold on, you just gave me a really interesting mental image... OK, I'm back.

These inject a certain mischievous sexiness into your texts that can lead to interesting places.

Another way to keep things light is to mix up your responses. Use animated gifs or memes on occasion as a reply. Not only can these convey a sense of humor, but they are often a way of bonding over shared interests. I've seen — and have had — conversations that were nothing but captioned Simpsons clips. You can even initiate silly role-plays and what-if scenarios and play them out to the illogical ending.

As always, the specifics will depend on your personalities; some people like wordplay, others prefer out and out silliness.

Don't get me wrong: this doesn't mean that everything is going to be jokey-jokes or that you can't be serious with one another. Someone who's always joking around and never takes things seriously gets as tedious as Stoneface McGee, who'd break into pieces if he so much as cracked a smile. But as you're leading up to the first date, you want things to be fun and engaging.

Don't Get Too Eager

Excitement can be cute, even endearing. There're women out there who can appreciate a guy who's the human equivalent of a golden retriever puppy — all excitement and eagerness and nervous energy.

Most women don't. And even the most adorable puppy gets to be a bit much after a while when it absolutely refuses to settle down. When you're all up in someone's face, peppering them with text after text, you run the risk of coming off as desperate or needy. It sends the signal that you're either lacking in self-esteem or emotional intelligence — both of which are unattractive qualities in a person.

When you're texting or DMing someone, you want to remember to pace yourself. One of the worst things you can do is go overboard and overwhelm the person you're texting with. Try to keep to one question at a time. Remember texting is a conversation and conversations are like tennis: you serve the metaphorical ball, and then volley it back when they reply to you. Firing off several balls at once means that they're going to have too much to respond to and, in all likelihood, decide not to respond to *any* of them.

While you're at it, try to follow the rhythm of the conversation. Every conversation is like music; it's going to have it's own pace and rhythm. Sometimes the rhythm will be more syncopated, as the texts are flying fast and furious in a back-and-forth that rolls like the drums from "YYZ". Other times the rhythm will be more measured, with time to breathe between each reply. The more that the two of you are in synch, the better the conversation will be. Just as importantly, she won't feel like you're that puppy jumping all over her and getting your muddy paws all over her nice clean blouse.

Keep The Compliments Non-Sexual

Compliments are another great way to flirt with someone —

part of the whole point, after all, is that you want them to know that you like them. Someone telling you that they think you're awesome is a great feeling.

The key, however, is how you compliment them. Not all compliments are equal, nor are all of them welcome, particularly from a relative stranger. 99% of the population isn't going to want to hear about how great their boobs looked in that dress. Or how much you'd like to run your tongue all over their ass.

In fact, the best thing you could do is avoid any compliments that talk about how they make your penis smile. Even telling someone how pretty they are doesn't necessarily make a great compliment, particularly when you have only just met them.

Here's the thing: most women have had a thousand compliments about their looks. And while they may well be proud of how they look — make no mistake, looking good takes work — most compliments about their appearance are essentially saying "congratulations on winning the genetic lottery." No matter how much work went into their hair, makeup or overall presentation, you're still complimenting them on something that ultimately wasn't up to them.

Plus: you have no idea what landmines you may be stepping on. Telling someone I liked her smile was all it took to torpedo that potential contact; as it turned out, she was incredibly self-conscious about her teeth.

Instead, a better compliment would be to compliment them on something they've had a direct hand in. Telling someone that she has an awesome job, or incredible fashion sense, or that she's funny tends to be a better compliment than how good she looks. These are things that she has accomplished through her own effort. By validating those efforts, you're saying "hey, I noticed this thing you worked hard at, and I think that it makes you cool." The fact that you a) noticed and b) think it's awesome are going to have a far bigger impact than being the 500th guy to send her the generic "I think ur hottt".

This doesn't mean you shouldn't ever get sexual or compliment her looks. I'm saying don't do it *yet*. You're not in a place where that would be appropriate or even appreciated. Wait until you've had a couple dates — or better still, a couple hot make-outs.

That's when the sexy flirting will be far more welcome.

Don't Over Text (Or: Respect The Ratio)

Texting is, by it's nature, intended to be short. It's a bite-size conversation, one that was initially limited by bandwidth, screen-size and the annoyance of trying to write words with a numeric keypad. The advent of messaging apps and smartphones with full QWERTY keyboards has made texting easier than ever before, but that doesn't mean that every texting conversation is meant to be an hours-long marathon.

Just as in-person conversations can drag on too long, so too can texting conversations. Even best friends can eventually get tired of constantly hearing the ding of an incoming text or the flashing Facebook Messenger notification.

It's very easy to overstay your welcome in a conversation with someone, and this is a great way to ensure that you'll never actually see them in person.

If you want to date, then your goal of getting someone's number is not have long discussions about the nature of life, the universe and everything. While these can be great, don't get me wrong, having long drawn-out conversations is more likely to leave you with a texting buddy, not a date.

One of the ways that you can avoid over-texting is to be aware of The Ratio. When you're messaging back and forth, the amount that you are texting should be roughly equal to the amount the other person is texting you. You want to keep things to a roughly 1-to-1 ratio.

This, for example, makes for a good ratio:

Hey, how do you feel about beer and skee-ball?

I love skee-ball. I used to make my parents take me to Dave And Busters all the time when I was younger.

I know what you mean. It was my dream to win enough tickets to get something insane like an Xbox or something.

> **Don't get jealous, but I was the skee-ball champion. I've walked away with literally thousands of tickets before.**

> Clearly we need to have a contest to see which of us is the master.

> **Oh it is so on.**

Both parties are responding with roughly equal enthusiasm, as reflected by the back-and-forth and similar length of replies. Everybody is interested and engaged in the conversation.

This, on the other hand, is a bad ratio:

> The Westworld event sold out pretty much as soon as it was announced, so I didn't get tickets. But two of my friends abused their media connections and got to go. Apparently it was freaking amazing.

> **Yup.**

> So I'm not jealous. At all. Really. Not at all.

> **Nope.**

This is a very one-sided conversation. One person is invested and excited. The other is only paying enough attention to be polite and — in all likelihood — would rather not be talking at all.

It's important to realize that this isn't a measure of interest in you, just in the conversation. There are any number of reasons why the other person doesn't want to talk right now. They could be distracted with something at work. They could be having more than one conversation the same time and have only so much bandwidth to spare.

Or they could be getting tired of trying to maintain a conversation that's been going on for too long and they're hoping you get the point.

When you start seeing the ratio start to shift against you... that's a good time to peace-out of the conversation, lest you overstay your welcome and risk damaging the attraction you've built up. Tell them you've got to do something else and you'll talk later.

Now this doesn't mean that you need to set an artificial time limit to your conversations; if the two of you are getting along like a house on fire, then staying in the conversation and letting it reach it's natural conclusion is fine. However, in texting as in showbiz, it's better to leave them wanting more than it is to ride that conversation all the way into the ground.

Ask For The Date Already

The single biggest mistake when it comes to flirting via text is when it never goes anywhere.

Yes, I know. You've dropped the clues in hopes that someone would pick it up already. You've said "Hey, let's get together some time" or "We should hang out soon."

Straight talk: that doesn't count as "asking someone for a date". These are weak invitations that give nothing for the other person to get excited about.

Sure, your mere presence may be lovely, but most people are going to want more than that. You need to give them a reason to actually be interested to meet up with you. "Hanging out" isn't an activity that stirs excitement, it's what you do with someone you know well already. With a new person, that implies lack of planning.

Worse are those who follow up these weak invites with "so... what would you like to do?" Now not only have you given an unappealing invitation, you've asked the other person to the planning. If you're going to invite someone out on a date, then invite them on an actual date. This means having a specific activity in mind when you ask them out.

Now I get it: asking someone for a date can be intimidating. But the fact of the matter is that most people seriously overthink the process and lose sight of a very simple fact: you like her, she (presumably) likes you and you both would like to do things together. Playing weird status games like "don't show too much interest" or "maintain a high-status frame" only gets in the way and leads to headaches and confusion. To paraphrase the sage, games never help, they only hurt.

While yes, you don't want to treat any person you barely know as your last chance forever of ever knowing the touch of a woman, trying to project the mindset that she's just one number in your harem is a great way to give the impression you don't care at all.

Inviting someone for a date isn't terribly complicated, nor does it need to be so intimidating. No matter how twisted up inside you get about pulling the metaphorical trigger, the process is much simpler than your jerk brain makes it out to be.

Here's all you need to do...

Just. Ask. Her.

Seriously. Anything more than this just makes things more complicated and risks getting people annoyed.

If you followed my advice and invited them on a date before getting her number, then you're two thirds of the way there already. You just need to work out the logistics.

If you haven't, then the best way to ask someone on a date is to stop hemming and hawing and just spit it out. Literally just say "Hey, I have an idea: let's do $COOL_THING at $COOL_PLACE at $TIME". It's that simple.

Now for some people this can feel a little too blunt. It takes guts to just put yourself out there like that. But that's the point. It's bold and it's direct and that's the appeal. There's no mistaking your intent.

Even better, you'll know where you stand with this person almost immediately. If they're into you, they'll say "ok that sounds great!" If they're into you but not available or not quite into the date you proposed, they'll come back with a "I'd love to but I can't, what about $OTHER_TIME?" Or they will suggest another option. As long as they're responding with alternatives, then you know that they're into you and they're committed to trying to make this date happen.

Now if you just can't bring yourself to be that direct, then another option is to pre-seed the date, as I mentioned back in chapter 2. You can bring up weekend plans, or you can just frame it as a question:

"Hey, how do you feel about go-karts? Awesome, I had an idea: there's this place that races go-karts, let's go this weekend."

 Combine ideas for interesting potential dates: get some wings and go play pool. Go to a local dessert lounge and see a cool band. Try a hookah lounge and craft cocktails.

Just make sure that these are all unequivocally dates.

Remember: you don't need to make a production over this or try to gauge her interest. If she's given you her number and she's engaging with you when you text her then you already know she's interested. All that's left is for you to take the final step and move from the phone to in person.

CHAPTER 5

The 7 Deadly Sins of Texting

The point of texting isn't just to text someone, it's to move the relationship forward.

Snatching Defeat From The Jaws of Victory

Almost any woman who's ever given her number out has dealt with people who've killed their chances by having lousy text game. There's the guy who can't catch a hint with both hands and a head start. There's the dude who's cute but dull as a brick. There's the guy who doesn't text so much as send novels, and the guy who seems to think "what's up?" is an invitation to tell her about literally everything he did that day.

There's the dude who can't spell, the guy who freaks out if someone takes longer than 5 seconds to respond and the guy who seems to think that getting a woman's phone number is an invitation to ask for nudes constantly.

The truth is that most guys are awful when it comes to flirting over text. The fact that you actually spell words correctly and don't do the conversational equivalent of leering and waggling your eyebrows is enough to put you ahead of the pack.

But don't let that go to your head. Doing better than most doesn't mean that you can't still end up ruining things with that sexy someone.

If you're suddenly getting radio silence from the people you've been texting with, you're going to want to make sure you're not making these deadly texting mistakes

You're Boring.

When it comes to dating in all of its forms, there's one universal sin: being boring. The worst dates aren't the ones where you and your date hate each other with the passion of a thousand suns. They're the ones where nothing happens and you're now an hour closer to death with nothing to show for it. So it is with texting. We only have so much time in this world and none of us want to waste it trying to pound life into a conversational corpse. That's time and energy we could be using doing more important things, like comparing toilet paper b rands.

One of the reasons why guys get ghosted and folks do the fade is that there's no reason to want to stay in contact with them. The conversations start duller than a butter knife and just get worse from there. Meaningless "just want to chat" texts drain emotional momentum from your interaction. The excitement she may have felt about getting to know you is going to die quietly in the corner when every conversation is some variation of this:

This isn't to say that every conversation has to be sparkling with wit and banter that would make Oscar Wilde proud to claim he said it first, but it does need to be interesting and engaging. There should be substance behind your texting – something meaty that the other person can sink their conversational teeth into.

I've given you a number of ideas in chapter 3, all of which help make you more entertaining and engaging than the "just want to talk" guy. Jokes, cool stories, even silly questions all help make you worth talking to. You could even be texting just to flirt, because flirting is inherently fun. But if all you're doing is killing time, then you're killing the attraction as well.

You're trying to build and maintain emotional momentum that leads to going on a date. Pointless conversations don't move you closer to actually meeting up in person. Pointless, boring conversations are where attraction goes to die.

You Have No Chill

The second most common texting mistake guys make is simple: they come across as being too needy. Whether they mean to or not, their behavior projects intense desperation, which turns people off. Neediness sends the message that not only do you not bring anything to the table, but you're going to make constant emotional demands. People have enough to worry about in their own lives without having to be responsible for someone else's emotional state.

This manifests in a number of ways. The most common example is the guy who's constantly texting and messaging. He's the one who will send dozens upon dozens of pointless texts at all hours. He can't stand the written equivalent of lulls in the conversation, so he fills the ether with chatter.

Remember, you want to keep your conversational ratio around 1:1. While there's always going to be a slight imbalance in the conversation – sometimes somebody gets on a roll – you want to treat it like tennis: one serve, then volleying back and forth.

This keeps the conversations from getting one-sided and – more importantly – it keeps you from acting like you need their attention.

Similarly, don't freak out when the person you're talking to doesn't respond within the first couple of minutes. Part of the beauty of texting is that you can take your time to respond, and that goes both ways. Just as you may want to wait to reply when it's convenient, so might she. If you haven't heard back within 24 hours, then you can start to wonder if they're ignoring you.

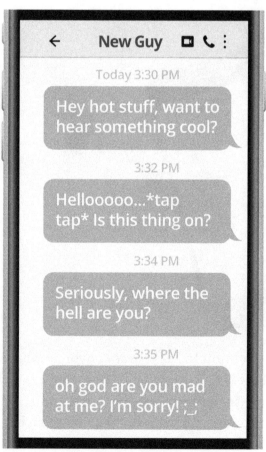

Like Gatsby staring at the lights out in the harbor, you don't want to be the guy who's spending his days hovering over the phones, waiting for the "Read" receipt and the "..." indicator to pop up. It's not a good look on anyone. At best, it says that you have no patience. At worst it signals that you've gotten overly attached.

Not everybody treats texting with the same priority. Sometimes people get busy and replies get a lower priority. Other times they don't have their phone with them. And sometimes people simply don't feel like talking at that moment and they'll get back to you later.

It's important to be comfortable with letting conversations proceed at their own pace and not read too much into silence or unreturned texts. Chill out and let it go. You can send another message the next day.

You Text Like a 12 Year Old

Let's be real here: you're texting. Unless you're already at FaceTime levels of intimacy with this person[11], your words are

---

11 You're not.

your primary means of conveying your wit and charm.

Men throughout the ages have been wooing women successfully with nothing but beautiful letters and witty messages full of ardor and enthusiasm, conveying their passion through text.

Nobody has ever gotten laid with "u r SOO hawut". And no, you're not going to be the first.

While there're are many different texting styles out there — and folks usually text the way they speak — clarity and coherence are the currency of written communication. You may be the Moliere of iMessage or the Oscar Wilde of WhatsApp, but if people can't understand what the hell you're saying, then all your wit is wasted and your beautiful bon motes are going to go unnoticed.

The myriad ways that you can obscure the clarity of your writing is almost infinite. The most common example is the cnstnt use of abbrv & #s n single letter rplz. We no longer live in a world where texting is restricted to T9 keyboards where it takes two minutes and nine button presses to write out the word "hello"; you're not saving any time with those shortcuts. You have access to a full QWERTY keyboard, so use it.

Similarly, overuse of things like "u" for "you", random emoji[12], action descriptors like *glomps on you* or Internet acronyms like LOL or ROTFL are more likely to be turn-offs. Using them

12 This especially means Japanese or teen emoji or expressions like OwO or XD. Unless you and the person you're texting are both part of the same culture, using in-group signifiers like this to anyone outside the group just makes folks look at you funny.

sparingly is one thing. Dropping them into every single text you write like you're spreading pepperoni on a pizza, on the other hand, just looks idiotic.

But most importantly, you want proper spelling and grammar. Proper spelling and goddamn grammar. Look, I'm not saying you have to have a copy-editor go over every single thing you text.[13] You don't have to write texts like you're composing a term paper. There's nothing wrong with a casual, conversational style. But constant misspellings and lousy grammar just makes you come across as though you're stupid. Every phone out there has predictive text and autocorrect. While typos happen, texts full of misspellings, run-on sentences and random abbreviations are going to kill that attraction deader than disco.

You Drunk Texted

There is no worse time to text someone — especially someone you barely know — than when you're drunk, high or otherwise in an inebriated state. This is a great way to take all the hard work you've been doing, douse in gasoline, then sit on top of it all and light a match.

13 But it couldn't hurt...

Inebriation strips away your judgement and your filter. It's how you end up thinking "You know, I bet she would like to see an extreme close-up of my urethra" or sending those unfiltered thoughts you've been having about thirst traps on Instagram. It's how you have long, rambling conversations that make absolutely no sense to anyone who doesn't speak your particular dialect of Drunkenese.

You're not Ernest Hemingway, nor are you F. Scott Fitzgerald or Nick Charles; you're not going to be coming up with scintillating pearls of humor while you're half in the bag. If you're lucky, you might rise to the heady heights of "drunk Tucker Max[14]". If you're lucky.

You're almost certainly not lucky.

Straight talk: booze, weed or even sleep deprivation aren't going to polish your wit or make you any more charming than you are when you're stone-cold sober. Don't drink (or smoke or vape) and text. You're not nearly as clever as you think you are. All you're doing is ensuring that when you wake up the next morning, you're going to spend half your day desperately Googling how to remotely wipe someone's phone before you see the "read" receipt pop up.

14 Google him, kids.

You Made It All About Sex

The bane of almost every woman's online existence is the horny guy with no boundaries. Whether it's on dating apps like OKCupid, social media sites like Facebook or plain old texting, almost every woman has dealt with guys who try to turn every conversation sexual... often within the first one or two exchanges. All you need to do is visit blogs like straightwhiteboystexting or Bye Felipe to see object lessons in what not to do.

Nobody, not even people who are actively looking for casual sex, appreciates getting propositioned right off the bat. There's nothing charming or refreshing or even that interesting about somebody whose first message is "want some dick?" Even people who are terminally horny want to establish a connection and see if they have any chemistry with their potential partners.

Rolling into the conversation cock first is a signal to others. Under the most charitable reading, you're someone who's so blind to social conventions and emotional intelligence that it's amazing you're allowed out of the house. At worst, it's a giant neon sign that you don't see the woman you're texting as a person. For all intents and purposes, you're signaling that you see them as an especially elaborate sex toy and you're hoping to jerk off inside them.

This is, needless to say, not a good look. It is, however, a great way to end up getting your number blocked — and possibly having a screenshot of your conversation posted to Tumblr.

The same rule applies with sending dick picks, incidentally. It's not a sexy way to flirt with someone, it's the electronic equivalent of the cat dropping a dead baby squirrel on your bed and expecting you to appreciate it. Even when the flirting is getting hot and heavy, dropping your dong into the conversation is going to kill things stone dead. There's little appeal in a disembodied wang; the sexiness of it comes in context and relation to the penis-haver. Trust me: she'd much rather see it with the rest of you rather than flopping around on its own. And even then, she'd probably rather see it in person.

There is a time and place for sending pictures of your package: when someone specifically requested it. And even then, you might want to consider having someone else take the photo.

Now, that being said...

You Didn't Flirt, Either

At the other end of the spectrum is that you're not flirting at all.

In its own way, this can be just as bad as being too forward. Not showing any interest is going to kill a burgeoning romance more thoroughly than chopping off its head, filling its mouth with communion wafers and burning the body separately.

Now, I get the impulse to try to avoid coming on too strong. You want to be respectful. You don't want to be yet another asshole in the sausage parade sliding into her DMs. But there's being respectful and there's being so respectful that you never say anything. If you're not actually flirting, then you're sending a clear message: "I'm not interested." This is how guys end up in the Friend Zone[15]: they're acting like a friend, not a potential lover.

Flirting isn't just about generating attraction, it's about showing that you're interested too. Women aren't mind-readers. They're just as confused and anxious when it comes to dating as you are. If a woman gives her number to a guy and gets nothing but respectful and polite conversation from him, she's going to assume that's all he wants. And while having someone to talk to is great, the point isn't to just have long and in-depth conversations about *Supernatural* or the *Grand Theft Auto* series. You are, presumably, looking to date this person. You have to let them know that this is what you want. Flirting sends a message that you like them as more than just a friend.

---

15 There is no Friend Zone; there are just people who don't want to date or fuck you. The term is used here as a convenient short-hand.

Now, as I said: that doesn't mean that flirting needs to be sexual to be seen as flirting. You don't need to go from zero to penis in order to send the right message. The best practices are still to go with non-physical compliment or playful jokes and gently work up to more intimate topics after you've met up in person. Even when you do bring up getting physical, you can do it in ways besides asking them to gargle your balls. You can use innuendo. You can play teasing framing games. But it's the flirting – not the sex – that's important.

You Took Too Long To Ask Her On A Date

This is one of the biggest mistakes people make when it comes to texting: they play it so safe that by the time they get around to actually asking her out, she's moved on. It happens more often than you'd think. Guys, especially ones with little social experience, don't want to risk rejection, They want to be absolutely, 100% sure that the person they're interested in wants to go out with them. And so... they wait. They flirt, but they never commit because they're never sure she's flirting back or just being polite. So they check and double-check everything she says. They make tentative gestures towards going out... usually so tentative that they go unnoticed.

In short: they do everything but ask her out on a date.

As a result, they start bleeding emotional momentum and the attraction they'd built up dissipates into a cloud of frustration.

The point of texting isn't just to text someone, it's to move the relationship forward. If all you want is someone to talk to, that's great... but if it isn't, then waiting too long works against you. If you're not moving towards going out on a date, you're just spinning your wheels and wasting everyone's time. You actually have more to lose by not asking her out.

When someone's given you their number, it's because they like you. That alone is an indication that they will probably want to see you. But if you're also having good conversations and they're participating in the flirting and teasing? Then you really have no reason not to ask them out. You don't need a special excuse for them to see you; you like her and you want to take her on a date is the only reason you need.

Don't overcomplicate things or make up a story to explain why you're asking. Keep it simple: You want a drink and would love some company. Would she be interested in coming? There's something you're going to do and you'd love to take her with you. Does she have any plans this weekend, and would she like to go do this cool thing? Give a couple of times as options; being flexible but having specific plans is more likely to result in a date than "hang out sometime."

Just remember, reaching the heady heights of "not the worst" isn't what's going to get you an actual date; it's just going to keep you from snatching defeat from the jaws of victory.

CHAPTER 6

Sliding into The DMs (Or: How To Talk To Women On Social Media)

*Don't talk about your dick,
don't show her your dick and
don't be one.*

DMs: more than just the guy telling you to roll for initiative

In my time, I've been lucky enough to make friends with a number of awesome women who've been in the public eye. These women have included cosplayers, fetish pin-ups icons, burlesque dancers, lingerie models and the occasional reality TV star. Almost all of them had careers that required a heavy online presence, bringing them in front of thousands of strangers every minute of every day, and being friends with them gave me a front row seat to the daily deluge of thirsty dudes who were trying to hit on them.

It was akin to being at the receiving end of the conveyor belt at a hot dog factory.

To be sure, this behavior isn't restricted to women who're Internet celebrities. Almost every woman with a social media presence and pictures online has experienced horny guys wanting to talk about how she makes his penis feel. Or they have had guys who precede trying to talk to women by going through her entire social media presence. Then there are the ones who just attempt to slide into a stranger's DMs and expect to get a date out of it.

I've taught a lot of guys about how to talk to women, online and in person. One of the most common questions I get from guys is "how do I get this woman on Facebook/Twitter/ Instagram to go out with me?" Now, if you've read my columns or listened to my podcast, then you know how I feel about using Facebook to try to pick up women.[16] But as social media continues to become our main form of communication, it feels incumbent upon me to give some guidelines on how to thirst online responsibly.

Here's how you can talk to women online without being a creeper in the process.

Rule #1: Nobody Cares About Your Dick

First rule of trying to talk to women social media: leave your dick out of it.

There's nothing more likely to get you shut down than mentioning how turned on you are by somebody's pics. It's not

---

16 Don't.

flattering, it's not validating and it's not wanted. If you're not somebody who already has flirting privileges with her — and if you're reading this chapter, you almost certainly aren't -- then she doesn't care how she makes your penis feel. Even when you leave out the online equivalent of catcalling, making sexual or even overly flirty comments to someone you don't know is going to be uncomfortable and unwelcome at best.

This includes comments on pictures that are clearly intended to be sexy, whether they were taken professionally or simply for fun.

Let me give you an illustration from life. My friend Arden is, among her many jobs, a sex educator and professional model. She takes pride in her sexuality and enjoys posting pics where she looks hot. In one picture that she shared on Facebook was a selfie of her taking a bath. It wasn't a terribly racy picture as far as such pics go — just a selfie showing her face, a bare shoulder and enough of the tub to make it clear she was in the bath.

Even so, there are always people who are going to mistake showing any skin for an invitation. In this case, shortly after posting the picture on Facebook, Arden had this exchange:

 Horny Rando
Got room for one more?
Arden No.

To be fair, this comment is actually fairly mild as such things go. Many women have gotten far more explicit comments for far less revealing photos. However, the issue isn't whether he asked her to fuck him, or even just implied it. It's the sense of entitlement that comes with it.

Comments like these carry a presumption of intimacy that doesn't actually exist. You are making the assumption that you already have a relationship that allows for you to say things. That entitled attitude is unattractive at best and a warning-sign at worst. Even a mild comment like the one above is going to make people uncomfortable coming from a friend[17], never mind a stranger.

However, even when the pictures are overtly sexual, most women aren't going to want to hear about your dick. A woman who posts a pin-up isn't an inviting you to talk about how you'd destroy that ass, any more than someone posing with her pug isn't inviting you to say "your dog's cute, but I bet your pussy's cuter."[18]

It doesn't matter that the cosplayer dressed like Harley Quinn looks like she's a deep breath away from violating Instagram's Terms of Service. Nor does it matter that this friend of a friend posted a picture of herself in a bikini on Facebook or this person you follow on Twitter blogged her party outfit with the deep cleavage. They don't want to hear about your boner.

---

17 The only exception is if you explicitly have flirting privileges with that person. And if you have to ask, then no, no you don't.
18 Yes, that's one I've seen directed at a friend before.

Period.

Is she showing off her body for attention? Maybe... but so what? The fact that someone wants people to look doesn't mean that she wants to hear about what people are doing with that picture. If it turns you on, great, you do you. But unless the other person's explicitly and specifically asked to hear about what you'd do with her, then you can assume that she doesn't want to know.

Want to talk to women and actually have them respond? Don't talk about your dick, don't show her your dick and don't be one.

Of course, this inevitably leads to complaints about how "guys can't compliment women any more."

In fact, I'm glad you brought that up, convenient rhetorical device...

Rule #2: Understand How To Pay Someone A Compliment (About Something Other Than Her Boobs)

Paying someone a sincere compliment is a regular part of flirting. After all, who doesn't like to hear that they're enchanting or that they're the only cactus in your garden? However, as we covered in chapter 4, most men go straight for complimenting a woman's looks. 9 times out of 10, this is a mistake. Under the best of circumstances, complimenting someone's looks is both boring and unoriginal. You're almost never the first person to suggest that maybe she could be a model or how great her legs look or her boobs. Even "you're hot" is lame -- unoffensive, relatively speaking, but lame. It shows absolutely no imagination, creativity or confidence.

Giving a compliment about women's looks online also tends to carry the unspoken "...so be grateful" appended to the end. Many, many guys treat a woman's attractiveness as something being done for — or at — them. Complimenting her becomes less about praise and more about giving their approval.

The other thing about complimenting a woman's looks is that you're signaling that you really don't know anything about her that isn't all surface. As with flirting via text, if you want to compliment someone on Instagram or Facebook and stand out from the horde of douchebags flinging their dicks at her? Compliment her on her choices, not her looks.

Telling someone that she's sexy is at best, surface. It's one thing for a woman to hear that she looks good from friends and intimates; these are people whose opinions she values. From a stranger however, it's noise at best. What would make a good compliment though would be to bring up the things that make it an attractive selfie. Take time to actually focus on the image, not the subject and work out how to talk about it in an intelligent and interesting way. The composition, for example; talking about how, say, the heavy leather furniture contrasted with the white robe and the red curtains conveys a lush, even voluptuous sensuality. You might mention the way her pose directs the eye or the way the robe accentuates her figure or how her makeup brings out her eyes. Even how the light falls would make for a good compliment.

"You've got great legs," on the other hand, isn't. Even though it's true.

Compliment a cosplayer on how she put her costume together. Tell someone her outfit looks great. Ask a good question about something in the photo, so she has something to respond to. Spend even five minutes learning enough about women's clothing to say something intelligent about it.

Trust me: if you can put in the time to breed a shiny Pokemon or grind your MMO character to the level cap, you can put in even a little effort towards learning how to recognize kitten heels. It will pay off far more than any comment about her tits.

If you're having a hard time thinking of what to say that isn't sexual, then think of it this way: if you wouldn't like your mom, your grade school teacher and your little sister to see your compliment, then keep it to yourself.

The other thing to keep in mind: save the snark and sarcasm for people you know extremely well -- the people who know you well enough to read your tone in text. Snark is the devalued coin of the Internet and sarcasm is a shitty substitute for wit most of the time. 99.999% of the population isn't going to appreciate it, even when they recognize it at all.

And while I'm at it: the "gentlemanly" compliment of "you have such a lovely face, you shouldn't have to show off your body" isn't going to win you any favors. It just says "Yes, I stared at your boobs, but you should know I didn't like it because I'm a Nice Guy." If your compliment can be followed up with "m'lady..." then you need to rethink it.

Rule #3: Don't "Um, Actually..." Her

Speaking of social media sins...

There are few things that women find more infuriating than the guy who assumes she's an idiot. Whether it's the guy who believes that he knows better and needs to prove it, or the dude who assumes that she has but a dilettante's experience, no woman has ever appreciated a guy who leaps uninvited into her comments or DMs to "um...actually" her.

Especially when she knows more on the subject than he does.

Or when he's trying to explain her own work back to her.

Or, for that matter, when he is trying to educate her on her own lived experiences. I have, no shit, seen peak mansplaining when a guy tried to explain having breasts to a woman.

Now to be fair: not everyone who dives headfirst into a woman's mentions like Vultan's Hawkmen to correct her is coming at it from a place of "silly female, allow me to educate you." There're plenty of times where it's a sincere, if awkward, attempt to be helpful. Guys are socialized to believe that fixing things is a way of demonstrating our value.

Hell, I've ended up offering unsolicited –- and ultimately unwanted -- advice more times than I care to think about. We don't mean to come off as condescending. However, the fact that you don't mean to be insulting doesn't mean that you weren't.

The other problem is that, much like #notallmen, leaping into a stranger's conversations because you can't stand to let a perceived error go uncorrected tends to be less about fixing things and more making it about you. You're busting through the wall like someone yelled "Hey Fact-Check!" and now here you come to save the day and impress the ladies with your brain's big swinging dick in the process. The truth is, nobody wanted you, nobody asked for you and just leaping in just increases the odds that you're going to trip over your wang in the process. Most people couldn't care less about the rando who thinks that people owe him a debate or argument or his belief that she shouldn't have done $THING that he disapproves of – whether it's her tattoos, her clothes, her hair or her lifestyle.

Do yourself a favor; reign in your knee-jerk "Someone on the Internet Is WRONG!" reaction. If she specifically asks for help or advice, then by all means, contribute. Until then however, you'll earn far more points to assume that she knows what she's talking about.

Rule #4: Don't Stalk Her Social Media

Another common mistake that men make when trying to talk to women on Instagram or other social media is seemingly the most innocuous: going through entire media timeline and making your presence known.

Sure, to you, it doesn't seem like a big deal. However, when I asked women on Twitter what social media sins guys commit that turns them off, the one complaint that came up more than any other was liking or commenting on every picture, post or comment she's made. It's the social media equivalent of stealing the TARDIS and trying to insert yourself into everything she's done since the early Ordovician epoch.

Your behavior on social media sends a message and the message in this case is "I have studied every inch of you, every moment of your life and now I know you better than you know yourself." Even the most benign of readings doesn't see this as "I worship the ground you walk on", it sees "My love for you means I have no concept of boundaries." The further back you go (or start), the creepier it gets.

There's nothing wrong with looking -- that is, after all, part of the point of Instagram -- but looking is passive and anonymous. The comments and likes, however, get her attention; it's a way of imposing yourself upon her and can make her uncomfortable. If you're going to like or comment on her photos, stick to the ones that come up in your feed, without deep into her account. Yes, Instagram has decided to forgo linear feeds and uses an algorithm that shows you photos out of chronological order. It's annoying, but everyone understands this, just as they understand that the newest pics get the most attention. By sticking to these, you won't be foisting yourself on her.

And while we're on the subject: the fact that you can observe her conversations *isn't* an invitation to join them. People frequently have conversations with friends on Twitter or Facebook and don't appreciate folks who suddenly need to throw their two cents in.

Despite what many people would have you believe, the fact that you're having a conversation in a "public" space doesn't give everyone in earshot the right to chime in. You may overhear conversations at restaurants or on the street too; trying to leap in is often incredibly rude. Existence isn't permission after all, and violating social contracts is frequently a sign of low-emotional intelligence – an unattractive trait.

This doesn't mean that you can't reply; much of Twitter is predicated on the conversations started between strangers. I've made lasting friendships with strangers because of discussions we'd had on Twitter... but these have been on posts they've made, not @ replies.

Remember: a post in and of itself is one thing; replies to someone else are another. Leaping into a conversation between two people can be jarring at best, especially if you aren't mutuals with at least one of the participants. Treat it like a conversation in the physical world; unless there's an overwhelming reason to join in, it's better to just observe.

Rule #5: Treat Her Like A Person

Honestly, you wouldn't think that this would need to be said, but it clearly does: treat her like a person. It doesn't matter if she's an Internet celebrity or just some cutie that you've had your eye on: she's a person above everything else. She's not an object for you to drool over. She's not a Goddess to be put on a pedestal or your dancing monkey who needs your approval.

One of the reasons why women — especially those with a major social media following — will respond to some guys but not others is because the guys she's responding to are the ones who've shown that they're willing to be low key and talk to her like a person. They're the ones who can give insightful comments, even on the most blatant thirst traps. They're the ones that she can trust to not get horny and try to turn conversations in unwanted directions. Those are the ones who get the follow-backs and who they'll talk with privately in their DMs.

Those guys are the ones who've proven themselves to be cool. You can be that guy too, if you can keep your libido in check and focus on being the smart, charming guy you know you can be.

You build relationships — whether friendships or something more — through trust and comfort. Most of the men she's going to encounter online are going to be pushy, obnoxious assholes. If you can be someone who has something to contribute and show her respect? That's going to make you stand out from the crowd. Showing her that she can trust you not to be a horny creep? That's going to make her more likely to talk to you rather than all the other people clamoring for her attention. And those conversations can become the foundation for something amazing together.

So when you want to talk to women on social media, put your best self forward. Be clever. Be insightful. Be respectful. Put yourself out there, and then wait. When she starts to pick up those conversational threads... who knows? This could be the start of something amazing.

CHAPTER 7

Texting FAQs

If you're unsure if she's into you, there's one way to find out: Ask her out on a date already!!

FAQ #1 How Can I Tell If She's Flirting With Me?

One of the more common issues when it comes to text is how often it can be hard to read tonality and intent. One person's obvious intentions can be somebody else's frustratingly obtuse and inscrutable message.

You, for example, know that you're flirting. The question then becomes: has she picked up on the fact that you're trying to flirt with her, or has she missed it entirely? And more importantly: is she flirting back?

To try to determine if someone is flirting with you, you want to pay less attention to the content and more to their behavior.

First and foremost: how much is she texting you? Is it roughly equal — or greater — to how much you're texting her? For that matter, is she texting you first, unprompted? This is a good sign; she wouldn't be texting you if she didn't want to talk to you.

Next: What is she saying? Are her responses very plain and straightforward, in a "just-the-facts-ma'am" kind of way, or is she being chatty and playful? Is she giving you playful shit and teasing you? Even if she's not overtly saying "hey, I like you", it's still a clue. Those are not behaviors she'd be engaging in with someone she didn't like.

For that matter, is she being a little silly and coming up with absurd situations or silly games to play via text? That's a sign that she wants to play with you.

Is she laughing and using lots of emoji? She wants to be clear that she enjoys talking to you.

Consider this exchange, for example:

> **Just over at my friend's house, eating ribs and talking about horse ejaculate, normal Sunday night**

> **Dear God you and your friends know how to party.**

> **We are now discussing various penises across the animal kingdom. Not really what I thought I'd be doing with my Sunday.**

> **Not gonna lie: that's more interesting than my night of binging Netflix and passing out early.**

> **Oh god they're googling Godzilla penises, send help**

> **Nope. I'm going to bed. You're on your own for this one.**

> **You abandon me in my time of need?!**

WE ALL FACE THE GODZILLA PENIS ALONE.

I WILL REMEMBER THIS!!

Even though the subject matter is absurd — animal dicks, horse jizz, and so on — it's playful and silly. Even if it's what's actually happening around her[19], it's still a sign that she wants to talk to you and include you in the situation.

Another sure sign that she's flirting: is she agreeing to go out with you? Then yes. Yes she is.

Just remember: if you're unsure if she's into you, there's one way to find out: Ask her out on a date already!!

FAQ #2 What Do I Do If She Doesn't Text Back?

There are two variations when it comes to this FAQ. The first is when she doesn't respond to you at all in the first place. The second is when she goes radio silent after you've been messaging for a while.

---

19 It was, incidentally. This was from real life. Her friends are weird.

Both of these are frustrating, to be sure. Unfortunately, it's also just part of life.

In the first case, she's most likely ignoring you. For whatever reason, she's decided that it's not worth her time to respond. It could be that she's not interested in you. It could be that she doesn't remember who you are, or assumes that you're a wrong number. You have no real way of knowing.

Ideally, you want to avoid this by texting early and making sure that she knows who you are — preferably in a way that evokes the positive experience she had of meeting you. This helps cement you in her mind as that awesome, cute, funny guy she just met that she'd love to see again.

However, if she's just not responding to your initial text — even if it's as perfect and charming as can be — then the odds are that she's just not feeling it.

In the second scenario, you were texting and things stopped. Maybe you saw the ratio starting to change as she stopped investing as much in her replies as before. Maybe she just dropped off the face of the Earth with no warning. While it's certainly possible that she was kidnapped by pirates or the Rapture happened and she was one of the saved, it's more likely that she lost interest and decided to stop responding.

In these cases, the usual cause is that you took too long to actually ask her out on a date. Either she got tired of waiting to see where you were going with all of this, or you took so long to get to the point that the emotional momentum bled away and now she decided to just ghost you.

Now, if it's been a bit and you've exhausted two out of your three unreturned texts, you could try to send a Hail Mary text. I've used variations of "Hey, were you just at X place on Y date? Because either you were and you didn't say 'hi' or I saw your evil twin." It's semi-obvious bait, but it tends to get a response, which gives you a chance to strike up a conversation again.

However, the best course of action is almost always to just move on. If she's not into you, there really isn't any magic technique or special text that's going to change her mind and get her talking to you again.

Yeah, it sucks when someone just up and disappears instead of telling you thanks but no thanks, your princess is in another castle, bye now. Sadly, one of the unfortunate truths of dating is that it's often safer for women to just stop replying. You may be an awesome guy, but she has almost certainly encountered dudes who turn into giant green rage monsters as soon as they hear the word "no". Some women have gotten threats for turning men down. Others have been physically attacked. As a result, ghosting may actually be safer for her all around.

If you're getting dead air, then let her go. There're millions of women out there, and it's better to go find one who digs what you have to offer instead of over-investing in one person who doesn't.

FAQ #3 I Didn't Get Her Number, But I Found Her Facebook. Can I message her there?

No.

If you forgot to ask her for her number — or to add her on Facebook or Instagram or what-have-you — then stalking her profile isn't the messaging equivalent of a mulligan. Popping up in her social media out of the clear blue sky is going to be weird and creepy. If you see her again, then you have another chance to talk with her and get her number. Otherwise, let this be a lesson to you: always remember to ask for her number.

If she declined to give you her number, then that's not just no but **hell no**.

FAQ #4 Why Does She Never Agree To Go On A Date, Even When We Text All The Time?

You're more likely to encounter this when messaging someone on Twitter or Instagram than if someone gave you her number, but if someone just keeps turning down dates, even when you two talk all the time? Then she's just not interested. Sorry.

This is especially true if you're getting what are known as "soft no's" — when she says she can't because she's busy (and she's always busy), or she's just not up for dating anyone right now, or just ignores the invitation, acting as though she didn't see it. These are all ways women will try to turn you down gently; they're hoping that you'll get the message that they're not interested without them having to make a fuss about it.

Here's how you can tell the difference between someone who's interested and life keeps getting in the way and someone who's trying to say "no" without hurting your feelings: did she suggest a different time? If yes, then she's still interested and the two of you need to work out the logistics.

If not, then it doesn't matter what you suggest; she's always going to be busy and something will always come up. You're better off either just being friends — 'cuz hey, friends are awesome and occasionally can introduce you to people who will date you — or let this one go.

Note: calling this behavior out isn't going to be helpful. It's not going to change her mind, nor is it going to make things better. All that's going to happen is that you're going to go from maybe having a friend to definitely not hearing from her ever again.

FAQ #5 I Have No Idea What To Say!?

First of all: don't overthink things. Your goal is to get her to go out with you sooner rather than later. Long, in depth conversations are great... after you two have met up in person. The longer you are chatting over text, the less likely you are going to actually ever go out on a date. That's cool if you're looking for someone to talk to; less so if you're trying to actually get a date.

That being said, sometimes it can be a little difficult when you're starting out to know what makes a good flirty text and what sounds like someone asking if they can lick the inside of your ribcage.

Here are a couple quick conversation starters that can pique her interest, keep her responding and — importantly — move you forwards to Goal #3: getting that date.

> Has anyone ever told you that you're incredibly distracting, in a good way?

Or

> Are you adventurous?

Or

> What are you passionate about?

Or

> Tell me something cool about yourself.

Or

> Hey, can you keep a secret?

(Actually have a silly secret to tell with this one)

Or

> When's the last time you've done $COOL_THING?

Or

> Saw this and had to share it with you

(send with cute picture, an adorable puppy, delicious food, whatever. Not anything sexual).

Talent is great, but it's consistent and deliberate practice that hones even the most fumble-fingered newbie into a smooth-talking devil who can turn numbers into dates like a medieval alchemist turning lead into gold.

CHAPTER 8

BONUS: Making It To The Phone

Most of the time, we like people who show that they like us.

Taking it from text to phone... or Skype or Facetime

Despite the fact that texting is possibly one of the greatest developments since Johannes Guttenberg decided to get punk-rock and bootleg the Bible, you will, on occasion, find yourself in contact with someone who prefers phone calls to texting. Or who may prefer Skype, FaceTime or other video chat services. In fact, one of the most stressful stages of having gotten someone's number is understanding that you are inevitably going to have to talk on the phone with them.

With your mouth.

Despite how much you may wish you could avoid this at all costs, how you handle yourself on the phone can make all of the difference between a number that goes nowhere and actually getting that date... or even that relationship, for that matter.

You need to make the transition from the person she barely remembers giving her number to into the person that she can see in her daily life. You don't want to just be one more stranger who's always asking her out; you want to be someone whom she wants to talk to, someone she looks forward to seeing in person.

And if you're dripping with flop-sweat and stammering nervously every time you have to pick up the phone to call a girl, you're never going to be that guy.

But hey, that's why I'm here: to teach you how to navigate this field of terror like a champion.

Warm Up

A lot of guys, especially if they don't have much social or dating experience. can feel somewhat intimidated by the idea of calling someone they're attracted to. I've been there myself, more times than I care to count. It's that moment of sublime absurdity when merely punching numbers (or scrolling through your contacts) spikes your adrenaline like you just heard a wolf howl behind you. Your heart pounds as the phone rings and you find yourself silently praying for a voice mail instead of a live voice on the other line.

Small wonder then that a lot of guys prefer texting to phone calls; you have time to compose a reply instead of tripping over your own tongue[20] trying to say something witty or cool in real

---

20 ...or your dick, let's be real here.

time and avoiding that dreaded seven minute lull punctuated by "So... anyway..."

If you're the sort of person who gets nervous talking to someone you like on the phone — whether it's for the first time or the fortieth time — then the best thing you can do is warm up before hand.

No, for real. I'm serious. Stick with me for a second.

Just as you wouldn't want to start running a 5k from a cold start or start pumping out reps on the bench press the minute you roll into the gym, you shouldn't try to get social when you've barely been talking to anyone all day.

If you get stressed out by the idea of making phone calls, then the best thing you can do is to prepare yourself by getting into a more relaxed, easy-going headspace beforehand. Instead of putting yourself through the stress of an awkward call, schedule a specific time in the day when you're going to call her. Then, around a half-hour to an hour prior to go-time, you call someone you do like talking to. It doesn't matter if it's a family member, your best friend, other women you're seeing, or a platonic female friend... you want to talk to someone you feel at ease with. Your goal is just to talk to someone you can have an easy-going flowing conversation with and limber up those social muscles.

Then, when the scheduled hour arrives, you say your goodbyes, hang up the phone and immediately dial her number. You'll already be in a far more relaxed and talkative mood than you would have been if you had spent the day dreading the moment you would make the call. This, in turn, helps ensure that you won't nervously stumble over your words or sit in terrified silence as your brain suddenly decides to go blank on you.

Assume You're Friends Already

One of the easiest ways to banish nerves and make talking to people on the phone easier is is part of an ancient and sacred art that I like to call "Getting The Hell Out of Your Own Way".

You start by assuming that you don't need to impress them or win them over because you're friends already.

Think about how you talk to your best friends. You're already at ease when you talk to them. Because you're friends, you presumably know enough about their day and their background that you don't spend much time on formalities and the customary 10 background questions. Instead of asking them about who they are, what they're into or what their day is like, you leap straight into an actual, easy-going conversation. You're not stiff or anxious to prove that you're not wasting their time.[21]

---

21 And if you are, you really need to get some better friends, my dude.

Now compare that to how you think about people you want to date. The very thought probably makes various bits clench up in pre-emptive fear, doesn't it?

One mistake that people make all the time is that they treat building a connection with someone they're attracted to as though it were some hellish challenge that can only be overcome by passing several charisma checks, finding the Unholy Grail and answering the Riddles Three.

In reality, it's far simpler than that Most of the time, we like people who show that they like us. We're social creatures; we want to connect with others. The number of people who reject genuine warmth, charm and friendship is incredibly, absurdly small.

When you assume that the person is going to accept you — not is likely to or might but will —then you adjust your behavior accordingly. You behave more warmly - as though you were talking with a friend, rather than a complete stranger. People will respond to that warmth, inspiring them to be warmer and friendlier as well.

Plus, you won't be as stiff and formal as you would be with someone you barely know, nor will you sound needy or try-hard by attempting to impress her.

How do you act as though you're already friends? Well to start with, you allow for multi-threaded conversations. Instead of dogmatically holding onto one conversational topic, you let the conversation flow and twist in any direction it might naturally go. Allow the conversation to drift onto subjects you might try to avoid if you were attempting to impress someone. Similarly you don't spend any time or mental effort worrying about what she's thinking; after all, you're friends already.

Now here's the clever sneaky bit: human relationships work on reciprocity. Remember what I said about responding to warmth? By taking the lead emotionally and treating her as a friend that you just happen to be attracted to, you'll be encouraging her to respond in a similar manner. And because your brain takes its lead from behavior, when you both act as though you're friends already, it will help build that connection almost immediately.

Handling Voice Mail Like A Pro

Voice mail and unreturned calls are an inevitable part of dating — in no small part because they can provide a valuable screening service. The last thing any girl wants is some guy who will leave 20 messages on her voice mail a la *Swingers*, each one more unhinged than the last.

When it comes to voice mail, you don't want to leave a long or tortured message, especially if it's that first phone call. If you get the voice mail on the first call, you want to follow the same pattern I recommend for a first text: nickname, a little humorous intrigue as a hook and your name and number... because hey, sometimes she really did lose your number.

One of the easiest, most universally applicable responses is something like:

"Hey $NICKNAME, it's $YOUR NAME. You won't believe what happened after you left last night, call me back,"

It's a blatant hook and — much as with texts — you may well be called out on it... but in order to call you out, she has to call you back.

If you're playing phone tag with a girl, then it's best to keep it short and to the point. **"Hey $NICKNAME, phone tag, you're it!"** works far better than **"Call me back pleeeeeease"**. The last thing you want to do is to reaffirm that she's not calling you back. You'll do far better with **"Hey, I'm gonna be crazy busy. Hope you can catch me when I'm around otherwise I'll call you later."** It establishes that you're the one doing the calling rather than putting yourself in a position of praying that she eventually deigns to actually speak to you.

Just remember: if she's not interested in you, badgering her with calls or texts isn't going to change her mind. Limit yourself to one unreturned call per day per day, especially if you haven't actually had your first date. Unless you have a very good reason — people are quite literally on fire reasons — you don't want to call a second time. Better to accept the silence and try again tomorrow, but again: only one call.

Just remember: One unreturned call or text could be anything. Two is a message. Three means it's time to move on.

Have Plans Before You Make Plans

There's one important question that everyone asks themselves when they're seriously flirting with someone: "What would my life be like if I were dating this person?"

This isn't an idle question; compatibility of interests and lifestyles is a critical part of making a relationship work. Any woman you're interested in dating is going to want to know whether she can expect excitement and intrigue if she takes a chance on you or if her future with you would be a never-ending string of nights consisting of arguing about Netflix and then hearing you complain about Hanzo mains in Overwatch while she quietly dies inside and wishes she'd gone out with that bartender with the lip rings instead.

Think about that when you're talking with her: what do you have going on in your life that lets her know more about you? You want to demonstrate to her that you live an interesting and exciting life — one that she'd enjoy being part of. Talk a little about what you both have going on that week... not what you want to do with her, but the cool things that you've got coming up that you're looking forward to.

You don't want to come off as trying too hard — you don't have to brag about how you and your friends are getting bottle service at this club or you're going to a super-exclusive party that celebrities will be hosting — but you do want to actually demonstrate that you have a life outside of work and your apartment.

Now, if you're not living that life already... well, then you'd better start, huh? Start making a list of the things you'd be doing if you were living the life you wanted, then start going out and actually doing them. You have an almost infinite number of resources at your fingertips to find the awesome things going on around you. Check your local alt-weekly newspaper, websites that focus on events in your town, even subreddits or Facebook groups to find all the amazing opportunities available to you and start going to them. The more you know what's going on around you, the more of a chance you have to be living a cool, exciting life. And then when when the "so... what're you up to this weekend" topic comes up, you'll have more to talk about than just angling for a date.

Instead, you'll be inviting her to tell you about how cool your plans sound.

And that will give you the opportunity to say "Yeah. You know, since you mention it, I'd love to take you..."

Afterword

There's one more thing that I want to share when it comes to texting:

Texting — like all social skills — is a skill, and any skill can be improved with practice. Nobody is born an accomplished orator or a brilliant writer. Even the silver-tongued lady-killers out there started from zero and worked their way up. Talent is great, but it's consistent and deliberate practice that hones even the most fumble-fingered newbie into a smooth-talking devil who can turn numbers into dates like a medieval alchemist turning lead into gold.

The more you put yourself out there and make opportunities to connect with people, the more chances you will have to grind out your skills and perfect your technique.

And as you do so, you'll find occasions when the "rules" won't cover scenarios or people you will meet out there. Your relationship with each of the women you're going to be texting with will be as unique and different as the women themselves. Some of them will want to have long, in depth conversations. Some of them will be cool with heavier flirting up front. Others will hate texting and infinitely prefer talking over the phone. Others will prefer more hybrid mediums like Snapchat.

That's fine.

Humans are chaotic and messy and as soon as you establish a

common-sense rule, you'll find hundredsof exceptions to those rules. The key is to understand the underlying structure when it comes to texting. As you get more experience under your belt, you'll be able to adapt your skills to every scenario you encounter.

Your text and phone game is going to be like a super power. Use it wisely and well.

Good luck.

About The Author

Harris O'Malley (AKA Dr. NerdLove) is an Austin-based, internationally recognized blogger and dating coach who provides geek dating advice at Paging Dr. NerdLove and his bi-weekly advice column "Ask Dr. NerdLove" on Kotaku.

He and his work has been featured on Nightline, Fusion TV, The Guardian, New York Magazine, The Huffington Post, Wired, Sex Nerd Sandra, Daily Life, Slate, The Austin-American Statesman, Austin Monthly, Geek and Sundry, Boing Boing, Everyday Feminism, Buzzfeed, The Daily Dot, The Washington Post, Kotaku, Lifehacker, NeilStrauss.com, The Good Man Project, MTV's Guy Code, The Harvard Business Journal, and many others.

Keep up with the latest from Dr. NerdLove:

TWITTER: @DrNerdLove

FACEBOOK: DrNerdLove

YOUTUBE: youtube.com/users/DrNerdLove

EMAIL: doc@doctornerdlove.com

Join the Dr. NerdLove mailing list: http://eepurl.com/ciQeDT

For more more advice on dating, sex & relationships, visit him online at www.doctornerdlove.com

CPSIA information can be obtained
at www.ICGtesting.com
Printed in the USA
LVHW110758111019
633803LV00009B/407/P

9 780996 377270